Mobile Search Behaviors

An In-depth Analysis Based on Contexts, APPs, and Devices

Synthesis Lectures on Information Concepts, Retrieval, and Services

Editor
Gary Marchionini, *University of North Carolina at Chapel Hill*

Synthesis Lectures on Information Concepts, Retrieval, and Services publishes short books on topics pertaining to information science and applications of technology to information discovery, production, distribution, and management. Potential topics include: data models, indexing theory and algorithms, classification, information architecture, information economics, privacy and identity, scholarly communication, bibliometrics and webometrics, personal information management, human information behavior, digital libraries, archives and preservation, cultural informatics, information retrieval evaluation, data fusion, relevance feedback, recommendation systems, question answering, natural language processing for retrieval, text summarization, multimedia retrieval, multilingual retrieval, and exploratory search.

Mobile Search Behaviors: An In-depth Analysis Based on Contexts, APPs, and Devices
Dan Wu and Shaobo Liang

Images in Social Media: Categorization and Organization of Images and Their Collections
Susanne Ørnager and Haakon Lund

Exploring Context in Information Behavior: Seeker, Situation, Surroundings, and Shared Identities
Naresh Kumar Agarwal

Researching Serendipity in Digital Information Environments
Lori McCay-Peet and Elaine G. Toms

Social Monitoring for Public Health
Michael J. Paul and Mark Dredze

Digital Libraries for Cultural Heritage: Development, Outcomes, and Challenges from European Perspectives
Tatjana Aparac-Jelušić

iRODS Primer 2: Integrated Rule-Oriented Data System
Hao Xu, Terrell Russell, Jason Coposky, Arcot Rajasekar, Reagan Moore, Antoine de Torcy, Michael Wan, Wayne Shroeder, and Sheau-Yen Chen

Information Architecture: The Design and Integration of Information Spaces, Second Edition
Wei Ding, Xia Lin, and Michael Zarro

Fuzzy Information Retrieval
Donald H. Kraft and Erin Colvin

Quantifying Research Integrity
Michael Seadle

Incidental Exposure to Online News
Borchuluun Yadamsuren and Sanda Erdelez

Web Indicators for Research Evaluation: A Practical Guide
Michael Thelwall

Trustworthy Policies for Distributed Repositories
Reagan W. Moore, Hao Xu, Mike Conway, Arcot Rajasekar, Jon Crabtree, and Helen Tibbo

The Notion of Relevance in Information Science: Everybody knows what relevance is. But, what is it really?
Tefko Saracevic

Dynamic Information Retrieval Modeling
Grace Hui Yang, Marc Sloan, and Jun Wang

Learning from Multiple Social Networks
Liqiang Nie, Xuemeng Song, and Tat-Seng Chua

Scholarly Collaboration on the Academic Social Web
Daqing He and Wei Jeng

Scalability Challenges in Web Search Engines
B. Barla Cambazoglu and Ricardo Baeza-Yates

Social Informatics Evolving
Pnina Fichman, Madelyn R. Sanfilippo, and Howard Rosenbaum

On the Efficient Determination of Most Near Neighbors: Horseshoes, Hand Grenades, Web Search and Other Situations When Close Is Close Enough, Second Edition
Mark S. Manasse

Building a Better World with Our Information: The Future of Personal Information Management, Part 3
William Jones

Click Models for Web Search
Aleksandr Chuklin, Ilya Markov, and Maarten de Rijke

Information Communication
Feicheng Ma

Social Media and Library Services
Lorraine Mon

Analysis and Visualization of Citation Networks
Dangzhi Zhao and Andreas Strotmann

The Taxobook: Applications, Implementation, and Integration in Search, Part 3
Marjorie M. K. Hlava

The Taxobook: Principles and Practices of Building Taxonomies, Part 2
Marjorie M. K. Hlava

Measuring User Engagement
Mounia Lalmas, Heather O'Brien, and Elad Yom-Tov

The Taxobook: History, Theories, and Concepts of *Knowledge Organization*, Part 1
Marjorie M. K. Hlava

Children's Internet Search: Using Roles to Understand Children's Search Behavior
Elizabeth Foss and Allison Druin

Digital Library Technologies: Complex Objects, Annotation, Ontologies, Classification, Extraction, and Security
Edward A. Fox and Ricardo da Silva Torres

Digital Libraries Applications: CBIR, Education, Social Networks, eScience/Simulation, and GIS
Edward A. Fox and Jonathan P. Leidig

Information and Human Values
Kenneth R. Fleischmann

Multiculturalism and Information and Communication Technology
Pnina Fichman and Madelyn R. Sanfilippo

Transforming Technologies to Manage Our Information: The Future of Personal Information Management, Part II
William Jones

Designing for Digital Reading
Jennifer Pearson, George Buchanan, and Harold Thimbleby

Information Retrieval Models: Foundations and Relationships
Thomas Roelleke

Key Issues Regarding Digital Libraries: Evaluation and Integration
Rao Shen, Marcos Andre Goncalves, and Edward A. Fox

Visual Information Retrieval Using Java and LIRE
Mathias Lux and Oge Marques

On the Efficient Determination of Most Near Neighbors: Horseshoes, Hand Grenades, Web Search and Other Situations When Close is Close Enough
Mark S. Manasse

The Answer Machine
Susan E. Feldman

Theoretical Foundations for Digital Libraries: The 5S (Societies, Scenarios, Spaces, Structures, Streams) Approach
Edward A. Fox, Marcos André Gonçalves, and Rao Shen

The Future of Personal Information Management, Part I: Our Information, Always and Forever
William Jones

Search User Interface Design
Max L. Wilson

Information Retrieval Evaluation
Donna Harman

Knowledge Management (KM) Processes in Organizations: Theoretical Foundations and Practice
Claire R. McInerney and Michael E. D. Koenig

Search-Based Applications: At the Confluence of Search and Database Technologies
Gregory Grefenstette and Laura Wilber

Information Concepts: From Books to Cyberspace Identities
Gary Marchionini

Estimating the Query Difficulty for Information Retrieval
David Carmel and Elad Yom-Tov

iRODS Primer: Integrated Rule-Oriented Data System
Arcot Rajasekar, Reagan Moore, Chien-Yi Hou, Christopher A. Lee, Richard Marciano, Antoine de Torcy, Michael Wan, Wayne Schroeder, Sheau-Yen Chen, Lucas Gilbert, Paul Tooby, and Bing Zhu

Collaborative Web Search: Who, What, Where, When, and Why
Meredith Ringel Morris and Jaime Teevan

Multimedia Information Retrieval
Stefan Rüger

Online Multiplayer Games
William Sims Bainbridge

Information Architecture: The Design and Integration of Information Spaces
Wei Ding and Xia Lin

Reading and Writing the Electronic Book
Catherine C. Marshall

Hypermedia Genes: An Evolutionary Perspective on Concepts, Models, and Architectures
Nuno M. Guimarães and Luís M. Carrico

Understanding User-Web Interactions via Web Analytics
Bernard J. (Jim) Jansen

XML Retrieval
Mounia Lalmas

Faceted Search
Daniel Tunkelang

Introduction to Webometrics: Quantitative Web Research for the Social Sciences
Michael Thelwall

Exploratory Search: Beyond the Query-Response Paradigm
Ryen W. White and Resa A. Roth

New Concepts in Digital Reference
R. David Lankes

Automated Metadata in Multimedia Information Systems: Creation, Refinement, Use in Surrogates, and Evaluation
Michael G. Christel

Mobile Search Behaviors: An In-depth Analysis Based on Contexts, APPs, and Devices
Dan Wu and Shaobo Liang

ISBN: 978-3-031-01187-0 Paperback
ISBN: 978-3-031-02315-6 eBook
ISBN: 978-3-031-00222-9 Hardcover

DOI: 10.1007/978-3-031-02315-6

A Publication in the Springer series
SYNTHESIS LECTURES ON INFORMATION CONCEPTS, RETRIEVAL, AND SERVICES, #63

Series Editor: Gary Marchionini, University of North Carolina, Chapel Hill

Series ISSN: 1947-945X Print   1947-9468 Electronic

Mobile Search Behaviors

An In-depth Analysis Based on Contexts, APPs, and Devices

Dan Wu
School of Information Management, Wuhan University
Shaobo Liang
School of Information Management, Wuhan University

SYNTHESIS LECTURES INFORMATION CONCEPTS, RETRIEVAL, AND SERVICES #63

ABSTRACT

With the rapid development of mobile Internet and smart personal devices in recent years, mobile search has gradually emerged as a key method with which users seek online information. In addition, cross-device search also has been regarded recently as an important research topic. As more mobile applications (APPs) integrate search functions, a user's mobile search behavior on different APPs becomes more significant. This book provides a systematic review of current mobile search analysis and studies user mobile search behavior from several perspectives, including mobile search context, APP usage, and different devices. Two different user experiments to collect user behavior data were conducted. Then, through the data from user mobile phone usage logs in natural settings, we analyze the mobile search strategies employed and offer a context-based mobile search task collection, which then can be used to evaluate the mobile search engine. In addition, we combine mobile search with APP usage to give more in-depth analysis, such as APP transition in mobile search and follow-up actions triggered by mobile search. The study, combining the mobile search with APP usage, can contribute to the interaction design of APPs, such as the search recommendation and APP recommendation. Addressing the phenomenon of users owning more smart devices today than ever before, we focus on user cross-device search behavior. We model the information preparation behavior and information resumption behavior in cross-device search and evaluate the search performance in cross-device search. Research on mobile search behaviors across different devices can help to understand online user information behavior comprehensively and help users resume their search tasks on different devices.

KEYWORDS

mobile search behavior, information-seeking behavior, user information behavior, mobile search context, search task, APP transition, APP usage, cross-device search, information preparation, information resumption, search performance, human-computer interaction

Contents

Preface.. xv

Acknowledgments xvii

1 Information Search in Mobile Context............................. 1
  1.1 Introduction 1
  1.2 Key Terms 2
      1.2.1 Mobile Search 3
      1.2.2 Mobile Local Search 3
      1.2.3 Mobile Application 3
      1.2.4 Mobile Search Session and Query 4
      1.2.5 Cross-Device Search 4
  1.3 Literature Review 5
      1.3.1 Mobile Search Context 5
      1.3.2 Mobile Search and APP Usage 11
      1.3.3 Cross-device Search Behavior 14
  1.4 Research Design 17
      1.4.1 User Experiment on Mobile Search (Experiment I) 18
      1.4.2 User Experiment on Cross-device Search (Experiment II) ... 23

2 Context-based Mobile Search Behaviors 31
  2.1 Mobile Search Strategies 31
      2.1.1 Mobile Search Information Needs and Motivations 31
      2.1.2 Mobile Search Query Formulation 37
      2.1.3 Mobile Search Query Reformulation 43
      2.1.4 Mobile Search Session Analysis 47
      2.1.5 Detecting Various Context Dimentions of Mobile Search ... 50
  2.2 Modeling Context-based Mobile Search 51
      2.2.1 The Relationship between Context Dimensions 52
      2.2.2 Impact of Context on Mobile Search Information Needs ... 57
      2.2.3 Impact of Context on Mobile Search Queries 61
      2.2.4 Impact of Context on Mobile Search Effectiveness 63
      2.2.5 Multi-dimensional Model of Mobile Search Behaviors 65

2.3 Designing Context-based Mobile Search Task Collection 66
    2.3.1 Extracting and Expanding Mobile Search Topics 66
    2.3.2 Selecting Context Dimensions of Mobile Search Task 67
    2.3.3 Relevance Judgment and Ground Truth 70
    2.3.4 Structure of Mobile Search Task Collection 74
    2.3.5 Comparison of Context-based Mobile Search Tasks with
          Others 75
2.4 Summary 76

3 **Mobile Search Behaviors and APP Usage** **79**
3.1 App Topics and Mobile Search 79
    3.1.1 Identifying APP Topics and APP Chain 79
    3.1.2 The Relationship between Mobile Search Sessions and
          APP Topics 82
    3.1.3 The Relationship between Mobile Information Needs and
          APP Topics 84
    3.1.4 Temporal Features over APP Topics in Mobile Search 86
3.2 APP Transition in Mobile Search 89
    3.2.1 APP Transition Probabilities between Mobile Queries 90
    3.2.2 APP Transition Paths between Mobile Queries 92
    3.2.3 APP Transition Patterns in Search Sessions 93
    3.2.4 APP Transition Intents of Mobile Search 95
3.3 Follow-up Actions Triggered by Mobile Search 95
    3.3.1 Category and Identification of Follow-up Actions 96
    3.3.2 Temporal Features of Follow-up Actions 98
    3.3.3 Follow-up Actions Triggered by Information Needs 99
    3.3.4 The Relationship between APP Transitions and Follow-up
          Actions 101
3.4 Summary 101

4 **Mobile Search Behavior Across Different Devices** **103**
4.1 Information Preparation Behavior in Cross-device Search 103
    4.1.1 Definition of Information Preparation 104
    4.1.2 Modeling Information Preparation Behavior 104
    4.1.3 Understanding the Information Preparation Behavior Model 107
4.2 Information Resumption Behavior in Cross-device Search 111
    4.2.1 Definition of Information Resumption 111
    4.2.2 Modeling Information Resumption Behavior 112

       4.2.3   Understanding Information Resumption Behavior 114

   4.3   Exploring the On-the-spot Search Performance in Cross-device Search . . 116

       4.3.1   On-the-spot Search Performance 117

       4.3.2   Search Performance of Repeated-query after Transition 125

   4.4   Predicting Search Performance in Cross-device Search 128

       4.4.1   Mobile Touch Interaction in SERP 128

       4.4.2   Predicting the Search Performance 130

   4.5   Summary 133

5   Discussion and Conclusions **137**

   5.1   Discussion 137

       5.1.1   Context Factors of Mobile Search 137

       5.1.2   The Relationship between Mobile Search and APP Usage 138

       5.1.3   Modeling Cross-device Search between Mobile Device and

               Desktop 139

   5.2   Implications 140

       5.2.1   Better Understanding Information Needs Based on Context 140

       5.2.2   APP Recommendation in Mobile Search 140

       5.2.3   Prediction in Cross-device Search 141

   5.3   Limitations 142

   5.4   Conclusions 143

References. **145**

Author Biographies **159**

Preface

Due to the rapid development of mobile devices, mobile search has become very popular in daily life, and studying mobile search with the goal of improving search support and services has been an active topic in academia and business settings. Current studies on mobile search behavior are primarily carried out through large-scale log data from a single search engine. Although these logs can adequately aid understanding of mobile information needs, search time, and search location of multiple users, there is a lack of investigation on the impact of individual user's social context, search motivations, and other factors during mobile searches. In addition, as more and more mobile applications (APPs) integrate search functions, users can use different APPs to conduct searches, indicating the need for two important issues to be studied with regard to modern mobile search behaviors: (1) there may be many APP interactions associated with mobile search; and (2) generic mobile search engines, which have been the main data source for studying mobile search behaviors, increasingly only reflect limited aspects of a mobile user's search behaviors. Therefore, it is necessary to study users' mobile search behaviors on various APPs and examine the relationship between mobile search and APP usage through aggregating log data from different APPs. Furthermore, as cross-device search has been regarded recently as an important research topic, the user experiments in this book can help explain device transitions during mobile search, the user's information preparation and resumption behavior in a cross-device search, and the user's search performance in a cross-device search, as well as develop support for cross-device search.

In this book, we study users' mobile search behaviors with three focuses: context factors affecting a user's mobile search, the APP usages and transitions associated with a user's mobile search; and cross-device mobile search behaviors.

In Chapter 1, we provide a brief introduction concerning mobile search and introduce our research design.

In Chapter 2, we analyze users' mobile search strategies, extract the multi-dimensional search contexts from users' daily searches, and model users' mobile search behavior. In addition, we build a mobile search task collection based on context, reflecting multiple context dimensions. Furthermore, we recruit experts to carry out relevance judgments for building ground truth that can be used for mobile search evaluation.

In Chapter 3, we examine the relationship between APP usage and mobile search behavior, including the relationship between mobile search sessions and APP topics and the relationship between mobile information needs and APP topics. We also discuss the temporal features of APP topics in mobile search. Because mobile search can be conducted through various APPs, we explore

APP transition probability and APP transition paths between mobile queries, as well as APP transition patterns in search sessions and follow-up actions triggered by mobile search.

Chapter 4 covers another user study that focuses on users' cross-device search behavior. We analyze and model user information preparation and resumption behaviors in cross-device searching. With an increasing number of smart devices, users can search across different devices. Therefore, we unearth the characteristics of cross-device behaviors and evaluate user cross-device search performance.

Finally, this book concludes with Chapter 5 in which we summarize our research, discuss its implications, explore its limitations, and consider future work.

Acknowledgments

We are grateful to those who participated in our two user experiments. In addition, we express our heartfelt thanks to many colleagues who contributed to this book, particularly Jing Dong, Yuan Tang, Fang Yuan, Lei Cheng, Aihua Ran, Man Zhu, Xuan Yao, and Shuguang Han.

Our research was funded by the following projects:

- "User Seeking Behavior Modeling and Search Technology Development Within Multi-Device Integrated Search Environment" (No.71673204) supported by National Natural Science Foundation of China.

- Wuhan University's independent research project (Humanities and Social Sciences) "Human-Computer Interaction and Collaboration Team" (Whu2016020) supported by "the Fundamental Research Funds for the Central Universities."

CHAPTER 1

Information Search in Mobile Context

In this chapter, we introduce the background, domain, and perspectives of research into mobile search behavior. In order to promote better understanding of this book's content, we also introduce key terms. In addition, a literature review is presented to give a brief explanation of previous work on this topic. Finally, we present the methods of participant selection, data collection, and data analysis in our two user experiments.

1.1 INTRODUCTION

With the rapid development of mobile Internet, mobile search has become increasingly popular and necessary in a user's daily life. Therefore, mobile search behavior has become a popular research topic in the domains of information retrieval (IR) and computer-human interaction (CHI). In the U.S., mobile devices have accounted for over half of the search engine traffic (Statista, 2017), with the same being true in other countries. According to data from iiMedia Research (2017), mobile search users in China increased to 647 million in the second quarter of 2017, and 41.8% of users were searching for online information through mobile devices approximately 4–10 times a day. Google (2014) also found that its traffic from mobile devices has increased more than from desktops.

Internet search functions originated on desktop devices. However, mobile devices have so greatly changed users' living habits that the traditional way of accessing information through browsers on desktops has not been able to meet diversified users' needs. Users today can utilize various mobile applications (APPs) to obtain mobile Internet service, such as searching for information, making friends, browsing news, and so on. Downloads from iTunes App Store, Google Play, and other application stores are constantly increasing (App Annie report, 2016). In addition, the data from Salesforce (2015) shows that people prefer using different APPs to interact with their mobile phones and access online information rather than using the web browser.

Nowadays, people own multiple devices—such as desktop computers, laptops, mobile phones, and tablets—and the functional differences among these devices have become blurred. However, every device has its own physical limitations, for example, the small screen and keyboard of mobile phones, the inconvenience of traveling with computers, and the limited Internet access on tablets. Additionally, searches are interrupted when situational contexts change and people have to transition between devices to resume a search task.

Although many studies focus on users' mobile search behavior and APP usage, there still are some limitations of the existing research. For example, there is a lack of a systematic analysis of mobile search context and research focusing on mobile search task design. Evaluation frameworks such as TREC, CLEF, NTCIR, INEX, and FIRE seldom have tracks specially designed for mobile search. In addition, although research on APP usage has been increasing, existing research lacks cross-analysis of various factors, such as search subject, search time, APP type, and so on, during the use of mobile searching APPs. There is also a lack of study on the transitions among various APPs in mobile search and how mobile search is influenced by APP transitions. Specifically, the follow-up actions triggered by mobile search and the relationship between follow-up actions and APP transitions have not garnered enough attention. Furthermore, previous studies primarily focused on the user's search behavior on different devices, while cross-device search deserves more focus, especially with regard to information preparation behavior, information resumption behavior, and search performance in cross-device searches.

A mobile user's search strategies play an important role in understanding search intentions and search behavior characteristics. In addition, in order to design APPs and services for particular information needs and mobile contexts, it is necessary to understand how user motivation and context influence search behaviors. Research on the relationship between mobile search and APP usage, especially with regard to the transition of APPs when searching on a mobile device, can help to detect mobile search patterns and to analyze the context, motivation, strategy, and other factors in long search sessions. This can contribute to more interactive APP designs, such as search and APP recommendation.

In the current multi-device world, there is a critical need to develop a theoretical and practical understanding of this relatively new search phenomenon. Therefore, with this in mind, we conducted two different user experiments to collect user search behavior data on different devices. The first experiment took place in natural settings to help us understand users' mobile search behaviors in daily life. The second experiment was a controlled user study, aiming to analyze users' cross-device search behavior between desktop and mobile devices.

1.2   KEY TERMS

In this section, we introduce some basic concepts related to this book, aiming to help readers more easily understand this research.

1.2.1   MOBILE SEARCH

With the emergence of mobile phones and mobile Internet, searching for information on personal phones has caught researchers' attention. Moreover, mobile search has also become a branch of information retrieval. Early mobile Internet content was mainly accessed by mobile web, but with the rapid development of mobile phone functionality and applications, users can search for information through various APPs.

The definition of mobile search is similar in previous studies. Gui et al. (2009) concluded that "mobile search means user submits query to search engine on mobile devices." Teevan et al. (2011) believe that mobile search is a search conducted on any mobile device. Besides phones, other mobile devices such as tablets also can help users access Internet services. Xu and Zhao (2012) describe mobile search as "using the search engines to retrieve information through terminal equipment, such as mobile phones." In this book, the definition of mobile search is similar to what has been stated in previous work, but we also define it here as the use of mobile devices (like smartphones and tablets) to issue queries to search for online information, through mobile browsers, and other APPs.

1.2.2   MOBILE LOCAL SEARCH

Unlike searching on the desktop, mobile devices have functions of positioning based on geographic location, which means that mobile device users can search information around their own location at any time. Therefore, mobile local search is also an important aspect in the domain of mobile search.

Cao et al. (2005) state that "mobile local search is a procedure in which a mobile user searches for local resources, i.e., resources that are in geographic proximity to the user." Mobile local search can meet users' information needs concerning near-position services, such as finding a restaurant or planning a traffic route. Miller et al. (2010) state that mobile local search "is a technology that lets people search for local things using mobile equipment such as mobile phones, PDAs, and other mobile devices." Teevan et al. (2011) explain that "local searches are searches for places with a regionalized geographic location; common examples include restaurants, gas stations, stores, or area attractions."

1.2.3   MOBILE APPLICATION

In the early stages of mobile Internet, users obtained Internet service and searched for information mainly using mobile browsers. As modern mobile phones have more functions, especially with the rapid development of smart mobile phones, users can utilize various APPs on their devices; therefore, search activities are no longer primarily carried out through mobile browsers.

In Oracle's developer's guide, Rodgers (1999) states that "a mobile application is an application that can run on mobile devices without requiring constant connectivity to the server." In

Arzenšek and Heričko's (2014) study, the APP is described as "an application that runs on a mobile device and is context aware." Kim (2013) asserts that mobile applications "represent the computing functionality designed to migrate across hardware devices at runtime and execute on mobile hardware platforms." Based on these definitions, in this book, we define an APP as any application that runs on a user's mobile device.

1.2.4   MOBILE SEARCH SESSION AND QUERY

Search session and query are two important and basic concepts in the domain of information retrieval. A search session consists of one or more queries. Spink et al. (2006) explain that "a session is the entire series of queries submitted by a user during one interaction with the Web search engine." Jansen et al. (2006) classify the search session "from a contextual viewpoint as a series of interactions by the user toward addressing a single information need." In Pavani and Teja's (2015) work, the search session is defined as "the series of both clicked and unclicked URLs from user click-through logs." Church et al. (2007) studied more than 600,000 European users' behaviors and concluded that a search session is "a session where the user has engaged in at least some search activity." Generally, users might issue one or more queries in one search session. Church and Oliver (2011) analyzed the queries in mobile search session and their information needs.

The queries submitted to a search engine can reflect a user's information needs and search strategies. Yi et al. (2008) categorized mobile queries into 23 categories and found that entertainment information was most searched for by mobile users. Baeza-Yates et al. (2007) analyzed the differences between queries issued from a desktop and a mobile device. As defined by Wikipedia, a "web search query" is that which "a user enters into a web search engine to satisfy his or her information needs."[1] Query definition is basically consistent, and one that we agree with is: a query is content users submit to a search engine or other APP in order to obtain information.

Query content is the information that researchers typically seek out, as it reflects users' information needs. Therefore, classifying and analyzing search queries is important in order to understand users' information needs and search intents. Shen et al. (2006) explain that "the web query classification (QC) aims to classify Web users' queries, which are often short and ambiguous, into a set of target categories." Agrawal et al. (2011) also believe that web query classification can contribute to improvement in search relevance and online advertising.

1.2.5   CROSS-DEVICE SEARCH

As mentioned previously, we live in an era where almost everyone has smart devices, such as smartphones, tablets, game consoles (e.g., Xbox, PlayStation), and so on. Faced with a complex search

---

[1] Web search query. https://en.wikipedia.org/wiki/Web_search_query (accessed January 18, 2017).

task, users may utilize different devices to search for information at different times and locations. Therefore, the phenomenon of cross-device search has recently garnered a great deal of attention.

Y. Wang et al. (2013) studied this phenomenon based on large-scale log data, and they define cross-device search as a set of seven tuples, including: search history, query before device transition, query after device transition, previous device, current device, search session before device transition, and search session after device transition. Montañez et al. (2014) also conducted a log-based study about cross-device search and define device transition as "a pair of consecutive queries issued on the same or different device" and consider that "cross-device transitions include a device change between consecutive queries." Han, Zhen, and He (2015a) studied the user's cross-device search behavior facing exploratory tasks, and Han et al. (2015b) explored using mobile touch interaction to support the user's cross-device search tasks. Han, He, and Chi (2017) also adopted the Markov model for observed cross-device search behaviors and their underlying search patterns.

In this book, we define device transition as "a pair of consecutive queries issued on the same or different device" and consider that "cross-device transitions include a device change between consecutive queries."

1.3   LITERATURE REVIEW

1.3.1   MOBILE SEARCH CONTEXT

Research on Mobile Search Context

Search context has been identified as one factor that plays a vital role in mobile search behavior. Kong et al. (2015) propose two types of short-term contexts—pre-search context and in-search context—and suggest that pre-search context triggers a search. Liu and Wu (2015) propose that contextual information, including time, weather, and emotions, influences a user's preferences on a certain point of interest. Considering geographical location and user behavior as contextual information, Kiseleva (2015) studied their influences on searching and browsing behavior. Church and Smyth (2008b) studied the user, search content, search place, and search time in mobile search. Gasimov, Magagna, and Sutanto (2010) divided contextual information into device information, user information, and environment information and present a simple architecture for adaptive mobile web page browsing.

Recent studies discuss the effect of mobile devices on mobile search behavior. Church and Oliver (2011) suggest that limitations in screen size and the type of interactions and input that mobile devices support play an important role in shaping the way mobile users use search engines. Kamvar and Baluja (2006) present the difference about query inputting on different devices. Park and Ohm (2014) introduced an integrated research model to examine user acceptance of mobile map services in mobile devices. Studies on mobile devices mostly focus on how screen size affects search behavior, such as map search behavior. The device types are also considered as one of the mobile search contexts.

Mobile Search Query Formulation

Previous studies about query reformulation have mainly focused on the identification of query intention to provide accurate query recommendations for users. Kamvar and Baluja (2006) found that the query characteristics of mobile search and desktop search are fairly similar, and they also examined the categories of search queries. Menemenis et al. (2008) present a query formulation automatic construction scheme based on users' contexts. The proposed system uses semantic metadata extracted from the article currently being viewed by the user to automatically generate candidate queries, thus reducing the obstacles a user encounters while filtering information or re-formulating a query. Salama et al. (2013) propose refining search queries by utilizing users' social contexts. They created context classifications of mobile search queries and query optimization and reformulation based on contexts. Yu et al. (2011) put forward an ideal query solution to mobile location search problems (Active Query Sensing), which can always suggest the best queries for users. The system has already been applied to the video search sector (Yu, 2011). In addition to studies on recommender systems offering query recommendations, some scholars have studied the possibility of guiding users to narrow the query scope with the aid of information retrieval systems. For example, Tsai et al. (2010) used the mobile terminal of Google as the experiment platform and found that users can obtain fewer but more relevant results by narrowing the scope of document type. In addition, during the rise of mobile search, Zhang et al. (2009) proposed a mobile query extension method based on related word co-occurrence in view of hardware limitations of mobile terminal equipment. J. Wang et al. (2013) analyzed search logs of large Chinese academic websites and illustrated characteristics of mobile academic search behaviors from the aspects of query, search time distribution, search session, mobile search equipment, and so on.

Mobile Search Session

Identification and classification are the basis of search session analysis. Scholars use different criteria in terms of how to divide a large amount of log data into single sessions. Generally, search sessions are segmented according to a time threshold. The time gap may be 30 minutes (e.g., Tingting et al., 2015; Teevan et al., 2007; Piwowarski and Zaragoza, 2007; Eickhoff et al., 2014), 5 minutes (e.g., Church et al., 2008; Vojnovic, 2008), and so forth. Additionally, researchers can divide data by using the IP address, cookies (Jansen et al., 2011), and so forth. However, there are some deficiencies in these methods since a search session contains many different user behaviors (Church et al., 2007; Church et al., 2008). Solely dividing data by the methods above may miss user behavior data, such as content correlation between queries, in a search session.

A search activity includes a set of events, such as querying, information retrieval, and feedback by the user and the system to complete a search task (Daoud et al., 2009). Analysis of user's mobile search sessions can more fully embody the strategies users adopt in the searching process, reflecting user behavior characteristics. Kotov et al. (2011) investigated users' cross-session behaviors, finding that a search session includes other events besides search. They conducted an analysis by combining search sessions with users' search tasks. Taking topical coherence of queries into consideration, Hassan et al. (2014) extracted search sessions from log data and analyzed features of query formulation, user click, user information needs, and so on; they assert that users submit multiple queries within a search session due to difficult search tasks and the user's exploring search. Hagen et al. (2013) studied search sessions from the perspectives of time, logic relationship between queries, and search task. Church et al. (2008) classified queries into several types, discussed query reformulation and recurrence in the search session, and analyzed users' information needs, click data, and so on.

The existing research about mobile search is mostly based on a large amount of search engine log data. Since the amount of data is so large and search sessions are determined by time threshold or IP address, these studies fail to identify users and ignore content correlation between queries, leaving a user's search session out. Additionally, existing research is solely based on a large volume of log data, resulting in a lack of valid analysis of user behavior characteristics.

Mobile Search Task Design

A test collection of information retrieval is usually composed of three parts (Cleverdon, 1967): the document set (which usually includes various news articles, journal articles and data, web pages, etc.), the search topics, and the ground-truth.

There are different ways to design the search topic. Simulating users' information search behaviors is common. For example, TREC set up 43 topics for evaluating information retrieval in the legal field through simulating legal complaints and requests in the context of a lawsuit (Baron et al., 2006). Another method is to extract search topics based on users' search behaviors in real settings. Raman et al. (2013) extracted topics to evaluate complex search tasks through logs of a commercial search engine. Ekstrand-Abueg et al. (2013) established the One Click test set through users' real search logs, indicating the effectiveness of the nugget extraction system. Furthermore, methods of extracting search topics from websites have been utilized by researchers. Carpineto et al. (2009) established 44 search topics and at least 5 subtopics of each based on Wikipedia's classified catalog and measured the effectiveness of their clustered results of the three prototype systems on a desktop, PDA, and cell phone. They found that clustering engines are a viable complementary approach to plain search engines, both for desktop and mobile searches. Li and Yan (2008) extracted suitable topics from the subcategory of a search engine and its search logs, then designed a Chinese web search topic collection. Additionally, there are other ways to design search topics, such as INEX, which asks participants to provide search topics.

Ground-truth refers to the relevant documents or relevant information of each search topic. The relevance judgment of a document is accomplished in one of three ways. (1) Manual judgment is the assessment of the relevance of topics and the document set based on personal knowledge and cognition of topics. This method is used to design small-scale test collections. For example, to establish the Cleverdon (1967) test set, the search topic designer made a relevance judgment between citations and references, and then five graduate students made relevance judgments on the search topics and documents of the collection. (2) Pooling technology, proposed by Jones (1976), denotes that, according to a search topic, search results are submitted by all the systems involved in the search experiment, and the first N documents (N=100) of those results are collected together to obtain a possible related document pool. Carterette et al. (2008) made a relevance judgment on the documents among thousands of topics of TREC through the pooling technology. (3) Interactive Searching Judgment (ISJ) technology (Esmaili et al., 2007) refers to the selection of a search engine to search a topic in order to obtain the first 30 result documents. Then, by judging whether the highly relevant documents rank top 5–25, the system continues searching the topic and relevant documents that are involved in the ground-truth if the answer is "yes." When the scale of the test collection is large, the two latter methods are effective at reducing manual effort. However, some researchers believe that the absence of relevant documents will occur in the process of utilizing pooling technology, leading to a biased relevance judgment. For example, Mollá et al. (2013) proposed a document distance-based approach to automatically expand the number of available relevance judgments when they were limited and reduced to only positive judgments. They found that evaluations based on these expanded relevance judgments are more reliable than those using only the initially available judgments. In addition, Ravana et al. (2015) explored exponential variation and document ranking methods that generate a reliable set of relevance judgments (pseudo relevance judgments) to reduce human effort. These methods overcome problems with large amounts of documents for judgment while avoiding human disagreement errors during the judgment process.

Tracks of Large-Scale Collections

Nowadays, there are several information retrieval evaluation organizations that provide large-scale test collections, such as TREC, NTCIR, INEX, FIRE, and so on. Table 1.1 shows some tracks of these four collections in recent years. The search topics of these tracks involve the domains of medicine, mathematics, patents, automation, cooking, books, legal, everyday life, and network information. However, few tracks of these widely known search evaluation forums are specially related to mobile search, except for the track of One Click/Mobile Click of NTCIR from 2013–2015.

Evaluation Collection	Track	Time
Table 1.1: Tracks of large-scale evaluation collections		
TREC	Clinical Decision Support	2014–2016
	Contextual Suggestion	2014–2016
	Federated Web Search	2014
	Knowledge Base Acceleration	2014
	Microblog	2014–2015
	Session	2014
	Temporal Summarization	2014–2015
	Web	2014
	Dynamic Domain	2015–2016
	Live Question Answering	2015–2016
	Real-Time Summarization	2016
	OpenSearch	2016
NTCIR	Internet/Search Intent Mining	2013–2015
	Medical Natural Language Processing/Medical Natural Language Processing for Clinical Document	2013–2015
	One Click/Mobile Click	2013–2015
	Spoken Document Retrieval/ Spoken Query and Spoken Document Retrieval	2013–2015
	Temporal Information Access	2014–2015
	Mathematical Information Access/MathematicaInformation Retrieval	2013–2015
	Lifelog Task	2015
	Question Answering Lab For Entrance Exam	2014–2015
	Short Text Conversation Task	2015
	Recognizing Inference in Text/Recognizing Inference in Text and Validation	2013–2014
	Cooking Recipe Search	2014
	Patent Machine Translation	2014
	Cross lingual Link Discovery	2013

Table 1.1 continued		
INEX	Social Book Search	2011–2014
	Linked Data	2012–2013
	Tweet Contextualization	2011–2014
	Snippet Retrieval	2011–2013
	Relevance Feedback	2011–2012
	Data Centric	2011
FIRE	Arabic Plagiarism Detection	2015
	Cross-Language Detection of Source Code Re-use	2014–2015
	Mixed Script Information Retrieval	2015
	Information Access in Legal Domain	2013–2015
	Automated Story Illustration	2015
	Entity Extraction from Social Media Text—Indian Languages	2015
	Shared Task on Transliterated Search	2013–2014
	Document Similarity Amid Automatically Detected Terms	2014
	Morpheme Extraction Task	2013–2014
	Named Entity Recognition Indian Languages	2013–2014
	Cross-Language Indian News Story Search	2013
	Frequently Asked Questions Retrieval Using Noisy Queries	2013
	Question Answering for the Spoken Web	2013

Although much research has been done on web information search evaluation, such as cross-language information retrieval, question answering, and Weibo search, it has all been conducted in the context of desktop search. The only task collection for mobile search is the One Click/Mobile Click project of NTCIR.

One Click started at the 9th NTCIR Conference in 2012 and was renamed Mobile Click in 2014. The purpose of One Click is to satisfy users as quickly as possible after they click the search button, providing them with important information segments and the least amount of text reading.

In 2012, based on the research by Li et al. (2009), the track of One Click selected four types of search topics: (1) Celebrity, which refers to users seeking news about or images of a celebrity; (2) Local, which refers to users seeking a local listing address and/or phone number; (3) Definition, which refers to users seeking the definition of a term; and (4) QA, which refers to users seeking answers to a question. Fifteen search tasks for each topic were designed, and there was a total of 60 search tasks. Celebrity and Local tasks came from the mobile search logs of a Japanese search engine and were selected manually. Definition tasks used the look-up term as the query, and QA tasks used natural-language sentences as the query, obtained from Japan's Yahoo Answers data. The four fields of the mobile search tasks are search ID, search topic, search intention, and search string (Sakai et al., 2011). In 2013, the track of One Click-2 refined the search topics as Artist, Actor, Politician, Athlete, Facility, Geographical, Definition, and QA (Kato et al., 2013). In 2014, the track of Mobile Click realized different language information retrievals, of which 50 tasks are in English and 15 are in Japanese. In 2015, the search results of search tasks in different languages were ranked and collected based on relevance.

In summary, most current research focuses on specific context, such as studies on place or other contextual influences on mobile search. However it lacks a systematic analysis of mobile search context. Although there are many information retrieval test collections, the design of search tasks in general simply describes the different levels of information need without the context. And the test collections for mobile search are rare. For example, there is a small number of One Click tasks, and these tasks are only in English and Japanese. The One Click collection only has four fields, without many mobile search contexts. To make up for the limitations above, we will analyze users' mobile search behaviors in a multiple-dimensional context and build a model of mobile search behaviors based on that context. In addition, we will design mobile search tasks in Chinese.

1.3.2   MOBILE SEARCH AND APP USAGE

User's Interaction with APP

Current research focuses more on basic features of a mobile phone's interactive search, and the duration of the interaction between a user and an APP is important content in this research. Falaki et al. (2010) found that the time users spent interacting with different kinds of APPs can last from 30–500 min. They also found that there are 10–200 APP sessions every day and each can last up to 1 hour. With closer examination of each kind of APP, it was found that the interaction with navigation APPs takes users the longest (Falaki et al., 2010). Jesdabodi and Maalej (2015) found that interaction with an APP takes the user an average of 64.85 s. Böhmer et al. (2011) investigated the interaction behavior of 4,100 Android users and found that the use time of an APP is 36.37 s on average, which is longest in the morning. Ferreira et al. (2014) found that 40% of users interacted with APPs for less than 15 s, and the interaction can be shorter when the users are at home or alone. In short, the time of the interaction between users and APPs is generally short, which is connected to the users' habits of using mobile phones.

The interaction between users and APPs has different characteristics in both number and type. This does not mean that users will use every APP equally as they install them. According to the different phases in APP interaction, Böhmer et al. (2011) summarized the life circle of APPs into five main factors: install, update, uninstall, open, and close. They found that users only pay attention to a few of the APPs they installed (Falaki et al., 2010). Falaki et al. (2010) found that 90%

of interactions are only with one APP, which means that users tend to use one APP to complete separate tasks and that one APP can complete most tasks. Jesdabodi and Maalej (2015) found that most interactions occur in social APPs, which is the same conclusion of Böhmer et al. (2011).

In addition, the user's context, such as time and location, could influence interactions with APPs and the type of APPs with which the user interacts. Similar to the usage habits with mobile phones, users' interactions with APPs are distinct based on the time of day (Falaki et al., 2010; Xu et al., 2011). This means that the frequency of interactions changes with the time of day and users tend to use certain APPs at different times. The use of communication APPs is equally distributed throughout a day, while news and weather APPs are used more frequently in the morning (Verkasalo, 2009). Social APPs, however, are used most frequently at night (Böhmer et al., 2011). In general, the length of the interaction between users and APPs is longer during the day than at night, while for some frequently used APPs, such as entertainment and multimedia APPs, interaction is active all day long (Xu et al., 2011). Furthermore, location can influence the interaction between users and APPs. Verkasalo (2009) found that the usage of some types of APPs (such as music and video APPs) increases when users are changing location.

Researchers also investigated the roles that APPs play in a user's daily life. Instant messaging APPs might improve the active participation of students when used in class or in other educational situations (Gan and Balakrishnan, 2016). At the same time, the factor analysis on the interaction with social APPs can help improve the efficiency of a ranking algorithm in mobile local search (Kahveci et al., 2016). In addition, another field researchers have paid attention to is the user evaluation on an APP. Knowing the user evaluation and improving an APP's user-friendliness is critical in order to attract users (Khalid et al., 2015). Fu et al. (2013) investigated poorly evaluated APPs in an APP store and concluded that the reasons for the poor ratings are incorrect functions, uneven operation, and so on.

Relation between Mobile Search and APP Usage

As users can utilize different APPs to access Internet services and search for information, the association between mobile search and APP interaction has gained more attention. Some topics of interest are: the type of APP used in a mobile search, the interaction between mobile search activities and an APP, and the transition between different APPs in the mobile search process.

The study of mobile search behavior has begun to explore the process of using APPs throughout the day, including the search activity of using a single type or specialty APP. Song (2015) found that users tend to search for more special topic information when using the specific types of APPs. Xu et al. (2011) found that even when a user searches for the same type of information, they use different APPs. Users tend to use many APPs, and browsing, social, shopping, and entertainment-related APPs are used most in a mobile search; after search activities, the users will continue to engage in a series of APP interactive activities (Carrascal and Church, 2015). In addition, the search behavior of users in a single APP will help to improve the design of that APP's function. For example, Hou et al. (2016) studied the influence of user search behavior on the design of a leading function in shopping APPs, which indicates that APP search function is helpful for enhancing user experience.

Users often switch between certain types of APPs, such as the interaction between news and entertainment APPs, tourism and navigation APPs, weather and news APPs, and so on. (Xu et al., 2011). Böhmer et al. (2011) discovered that the highest probability that users will utilize instant message APPs is after a mobile search. Carrascal and Church (2015) analyzed "application chain (APP chain)" in the process of mobile phone usage, finding that frequent APP interactions could trigger mobile search activity, but failed to discuss the relationship between mobile search and APP transition.

Researchers have also begun to predict APP transition using the context model method (Shin, Hong and Dey, 2012) and historical interaction log data (Gouin-Vallerand and Mezghani, 2014).

APP Transitions in Mobile Search

Carrascal and Church (2015) studied the transitions between APPs and explored the causes through a qualitative study. They found that users tend to engage in sharing actions after searching with different APPs. They believe that transitions between APPs are caused by different activities on the mobile device. Wu and Liang (2016) also found that users might make purchases, share information, and continue searching on different APPs after initial queries.

Researchers have also explored the prediction of APP transition during smartphone usage. The context model, which collects a wide range of contextual information on the mobile device, can contribute to predicting APP usages (Shin, Hong and Dey, 2012), and the historical data of the user's interaction also can be applied to studying APP transition (Gouin-Vallerand and Mezghani, 2014).

In the search process, users may interact more with mobile devices and engage in actual activities that could be seen as follow-up actions triggered by a mobile search. Some commercial organizations have also studied the conversion of mobile search to actual activities. They studied the follow-up actions of mobile search from the perspective of the types of actions, time expended for conversion, and so on. Google, IpsosMediaCT, and Purchased (2014) investigated consumer's search behavior and found that half of the mobile phone users would visit the store they had searched for, which is similar to the results of Teevan's study (2011). Google and Nielsen (2013) focused on the conversion of mobile search, finding that 73% of mobile searches will lead to actual activities, such as continuing a search, visiting a website, sharing information, visiting a store, shopping, calling, and so on. Neustar (2014) surveyed cross-device search behavior and found that the conversion rate of mobile search is the highest, especially when users search for local information.

The main methods used are network questionnaire and/or interview survey, without the support of objective mobile usage data.

On the whole, current research has paid more attention to information needs, type of APP used, and other behavioral characteristics, as well as descriptive analysis of the other APP interaction phenomena that appear in the user's mobile search process. There is a lack of study on the transitions among various APPs during a mobile search and how mobile search is influenced by APP transitions. In addition, the studies of activities triggered by mobile search mainly focus on the connection between mobile search and consumption, and there is a lack of deep academic research and analysis on the follow-up actions of mobile search, especially for specific groups like college students, and the causes of such actions.

1.3.3   CROSS-DEVICE SEARCH BEHAVIOR

Cross-session and Cross-device Search

Current studies have focused not only on single-session search behaviors, but also on cross-session search behaviors. There is an abundance of existing findings that show that a complicated search task spans a long time, when users need to search in one continuous session or multiple sessions. Therefore, the cross-session web search has been defined (Kotov et al., 2011; Agichtein et al., 2012; Wang, H. et al., 2013). There is some research on identifying and extracting cross-session search tasks, through the method of modeling cross-session search behaviors. H. Wang et al. (2013) provide a way to identify long-term and cross-session search tasks by investigating inter-query dependencies learned from users' searching behaviors. They proposed a semi-supervised clustering model based on the latent structural SVM model, and a set of effective automatic annotation rules were proposed as weak supervision to release the burden of manual annotation. Kotov et al. (2011) proposed methods for modeling and analyzing user search behaviors extending over multiple search sessions, addressing the challenge of identifying all previous queries on the same search task and predicting whether a user would return to the task in future sessions. They developed two classifiers, Logistic Regression (LR) and Multiple Additive Regression Trees (MART), for these two tasks. It was shown that these classifiers can perform both tasks effectively, using labeled data from search logs.

It stands to reason that, as long as people search on different devices, cross-device search will be a topic of research (Wang Y. et al., 2013; Montañez et al., 2014; Han et al., 2015a). However, studies have shown that user activities tend to span multiple devices (Aula et al., 2005), and dissatisfying experiences on mobile devices drive users to complete their tasks on desktops (Karlson et al., 2010). Transitioning between devices necessitates the switching of sessions; cross-device search is a special case of cross-session search. Some research concentrates on analyzing cross-device search behaviors and patterns based on large-scale search logs from commercial search engines. Y. Wang et al. (2013) present a log-based study to define and characterize cross-device search behaviors and predict the resumption of cross-device tasks. They show that there are discernible and noteworthy patterns of search behaviors associated with device transitions. However, this result was concluded within the circumstance of transitioning from a PC to a smartphone and with a particular definition of the search task. Montañez et al. (2014) formalized the cross-device search and examined a general scenario of cross-device search with four types of devices, including gaming consoles. They characterized transitions between devices, detected device transitions, and predicted target devices. Other research on supporting cross-session and cross-device search experiences is also relevant, as it provides interface-level and algorithm-level support. Han et al. (2015a, 2015b, 2017) have provided many studies in the domain of cross-device search. They analyzed users' behavioral patterns and compared them with the patterns in desktop-to-desktop web search. Additionally, they (2015a and 2015b) examined several approaches using Mobile Touch Interactions (MTIs) to infer relevant content so that such content could be used for supporting subsequent search queries on desktop computers. Han, He, and Chi (2017) also modeled the observed cross-device search behaviors and their underlying search patterns.

Task Interruption and Task Resumption

Early research shows that 40% of individuals' information tasks cannot be completed in a single session, mainly due to interruption (Sellen et al., 2002). In cross-device search, search sessions that resume after switching devices are a recovery or continuation of the initial search. Users will then rebuild the search memory. The results of some research demonstrate the existence of task resumption behavior in cross-session search. Task difficulty, the duration of the task, the amount of interference, and other factors affect the user's willingness to resume the task (Czerwinski et al., 2004) Moreover, users submit a repeated query (Teevan et al., 2007; Han et al., 2015a) and re-view the same web pages (Tyler and Teevan, 2010) to recover their previous query status. These behaviors are referred to as task resumption (Teevan et al., 2007; Wang, H. et al., 2013) or multitask continuum in cross-session and cross-device search. Also, re-finding behaviors occur during task resumption of cross-session search. Teevan et al. (2007) showed, via query log analysis, that nearly 40% of queries are attempts to re-find previously encountered results. Tyler and Teevan (2010) also looked into the differences between cross-session and within-session information re-finding behaviors and discovered that within-session re-finding tends to involve re-evaluation, while cross-session re-finding tends to involve task resumption. All of these analyses examine queries that users submit repeatedly in cross-session search and show the phenomenon of repeated query and reviewed web pages, but none generate a relative usage model. Therefore, our research focuses on cross-device search and characterizes users' information behaviors rather than describing task resumption.

Performance in Cross-device Search

Research on cross-device search focuses on users' behaviors and behavior prediction and compares different device-transition directions. The main statistics come from search logs, including search history, click stream data, touch interaction data, and eye movement data. The most frequently used methods include statistics, machine learning, and so on. In the studies of users' behavior patterns, Y. Wang et al. (2013) examined search time, geospatial characteristics, and search topics and found that, for example, users are more likely to begin transition (leave the desktop) around 4–5 PM. Montañez et al. (2014) studied device-transition direction and found that device transition was mostly from mobile to desktop.

Studies on performance in cross-device search are limited, and studies about behavior prediction often involve search performance. Y. Wang et al. (2013) used accuracy, precision, and recall to develop search task-resuming prediction. They propose model features from five perspectives: search history, pre-transition session feature, pre-transition query, transition, and post-transition session feature. Their model outperforms the baseline system (desktop-only search), and precision and recall were better than the baseline system. Montañez et al. (2014) developed models to predict device transition. They used accuracy, average precision, and average recall to evaluate the efficiency of their models. Han et al. (2015a) explored the usefulness of the MTIs on search engine result pages (SERPs) on improving search performance. They also used MAP and NDCG@20 to evaluate usefulness (Han et al., 2015b). Based on previous literature, it was found that precision, recall, accuracy, and normalized discounted cumulative gain (nDCG) are frequently used to measure search performance.

In addition, there is a lack of research concerning on-the-spot search performance, as researchers prefer to study on-the-spot search behavior and search systems. Jansen et al. studied users' real-time search behavior from three perspectives: queries, topic, and economic value (Jansen et al., 2011, 2010). Cui et al. (2008) proposed a real-time image search engine by re-ranking the search results. Their re-ranking method is better at improving precision. Zhu et al. (2017) presented a novel real-time, personalized Twitter search. They used latency-discounted gain (ELG), normalized cumulative gain (nCG), and nDCG as the metrics to evaluate search performance. In a web search, dynamic changes of search performance are hard to catch. In normal web search, it is meaningless to present on-the-spot changes of search performance. However, in cross-device search, device transition interrupts the search process, which may affect users' search performance. After device transition, it is unknown how users' search performance changes when they try to resume search tasks and whether it is a slow process or not. For these reasons, we use on-the-spot search performance to show dynamic change.

Predicting the Search Performance in Cross-device Search

Predicting search performance can contribute to improving user experience of search engines. Dwell time and query features are commonly used for prediction (Guo et al., 2013a; Fox et al., 2005). Kim et al. (2013) developed a model capable of predicting search performance by mining query associations.

On the other hand, mouse cursor movement and clicks are regarded as implicit indicators of search performance (Claypool et al., 2001; Fox et al., 2005; Joachims et al., 2007). Some explicit interactions such as highlighting and annotation are considered to be features of explicit indicators (Ahn et al., 2008). The availability of eye-tracking, scanning path, viewpoint time, and so on also play an important role in predicting search performance. Y. Li et al. (2017) focused on building a prediction model that can infer users' interest ratings from attention metrics.

Y. Wang et al. (2013) predicted task resumption using behavioral, topical, geospatial, and temporal features. Kotov et al. (2011) predicted whether or not the user will return to the current task in the future according to queries, search, sessions, and historical features. Montañez et al. (2014) proposed models to predict aspects of cross-device search transitions and the next device used for search using device information, query length, and so on. Predicting search performance is an important aspect of information retrieval, especially in cross-device search. Han et al. (2015a) depended on the MTIs obtained from SERPs and subdocument to predict document quality.

In summary, as outlined above, cross-session and cross-device search have been studied by large-scale search engine logs, which lack a specific focus on the research after a device transition. Furthermore, previous studies concentrate on predicting the device switch, the next device in cross-device search, and exacting search tasks in cross-session search. However, going forward, we will focus on the phase of cross-device search and descriptions of users' behavior in detail. Most studies focus on predicting search performance by various features in a single device search. However, little is known about how MTIs on SERPs affect search performance in a cross-device search. Unlike with existing studies, we aim to predict search performance in cross-device searches. Moreover, we are only concerned with mobile touch interactions on cross-device SERPs.

1.4   RESEARCH DESIGN

In order to analyze contextual influences on mobile search and to build the context-based mobile search model, we designed a user study in natural settings to collect users' real mobile search context information for 15 days without any interruption. This ensures the integrity and reality of the data. In order to understand and model users' cross-device search behaviors, as well as predict search performance, we designed another user experiment in the laboratory environment to collect users' behavior data from different devices.

Chapters 2 and 3 are based on the user experiment on mobile search (Experiment I), and Experiment II contributes to the analysis in Chapter 4.

1.4.1   USER EXPERIMENT ON MOBILE SEARCH (EXPERIMENT I)

Experiment Settings

In order to understand users' real information needs, search habits, search tasks, and mobile search context information, we designed an uncontrolled user experiment in their natural settings over the course of 15 days. In this experiment, we did not set any restrictions as to the kind of mobile phone, system, search time, search task, and so forth, that could be utilized by the users. Users could search any topic of information that they needed, helping to show users' real mobile search behavior.

Before the experiment, we investigated the search frequency, search habits, and background information of college students. Then we chose 30 college students who performed a mobile search at least once per day to be the participants to ensure the adequacy of the dataset.

During the 15-day experiment, we used a mobile phone logging application to collect the users' mobile phone usage data. To avoid privacy issues, each participant signed an agreement to ensure only the data elements would be recorded during the experiment, not any sensitive or personal information such as voice input, accounts and passwords, messages received, and so on. We also required the participants to fill in a structured diary each day to describe which mobile search left the deepest impression, with each having to report one memorable search task per day. This helped us to extract deeper dimension from the users' mobile search contexts. In the end, we paid 300 RMB to each participant as compensation for their work.

After the 15-day experiment, we conducted a user interview to investigate the factors influencing participants' mobile search, such as the reasons for changing APPs. In addition, based on the multi-dimensional mobile search contexts extracted from the 15-day experiment, we designed mobile search task collections. The procedure for the experiment is shown in Figure 1.1.

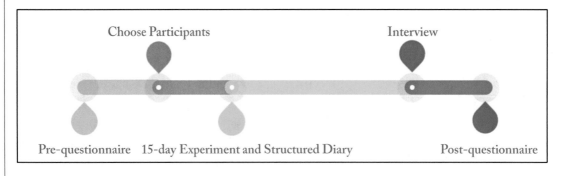

Figure 1.1: Experiment procedure for mobile search behavior (Experiment I).

Data Collection

(i) Mobile Phone Log

Large-scale logs often consist of the users' mobile search behavior data in a single mobile search engine, failing to completely cover all mobile search behavior on a smartphone. By installing AWARE, an Android framework for logging and sharing mobile context information, on participants' smartphones, we were able to collect complete daily phone use logs. After signing our agreement, participants were asked to promise that they would do a mobile search at least once per day. Each of the three laboratory personnel engaged in the experiment managed 10 participants. They checked the log records every day to ensure that there was no discontinuity of the AWARE framework and that each participant made daily searches.

Before the experiment, there were short periods of trial operation to test AWARE's function and output. System operation, application usage, keyboard input, and location information were recorded in the experiment. Since AWARE only records keyboard input, which participants could control, there was no privacy issue. Because we told the participants what kind of data we collected, they were reassured regarding the privacy of their data.

(ii) Structured Diary

Structured diaries were distributed to participants by laboratory personnel every day in which they were to identify the most memorable search each day. Information needs, information-seeking motivations, search sites, and contexts were requested in the structured diary, as well as any interruption of the mobile search session. The outline of questions in the structured diaries is shown in Figure 1.2.

Structured Diary in a Mobile Search

1. Your user ID in our experiment:
2. Date:
3. What were your information needs in this mobile search? (*Such as searching for a movie*)
4. What was your search motivation in this mobile search? (*Multiple-choice question*)
5. Where did you conduct this mobile search? (*Multiple-choice question*)
6. Did you change to another device to search in the mobile search process? If you changed, which type of devices did you transit to? (*Multiple-choice question*)
7. How many APPs did you use in this mobile search? (*Single-choice question*)
8. Were there interruptions in this mobile search process? (*Single-choice question*)
9. What was the social environment in this mobile search? (*Single-choice question*)
10. What were you doing in this mobile search? (*Single-choice question*)
11. Was the information you searched for important or urgent? (*Single-choice question*)
12. How did you feel about the search tool you used in this mobile search? (*Single-choice question*)
13. Did this mobile search change your feelings? (*Single-choice question*)
14. Was this mobile search successful? (*Single-choice question*)
15. If you failed in this mobile search, will you continue to search for information? (*Single-choice question*)

Figure 1.2: The outline of questions in structured diaries.

(iii) User Interview

As AWARE only records objective data of the use of mobile phones, we conducted semi-structured interviews with participants to investigate factors and causes of the behavioral characteristics. The interviews mainly concentrated on those searches recorded by the participants with which they were the most impressed. Some participants' utterances, collected during the interviews, were translated from Chinese to English due to privacy protection and to help readers to understand. This helped illuminate the factors that were not recorded by AWARE.

The interview questions mainly focused on the reasons behind the users' behavior, such as: Why did the user change to another APP to search for information? Why did the user change to another device in the mobile search? Why did the user search for another topic of information after the initial query?

(iv) Post-questionnaire

Due to the small sample of users' real search tasks extracted from the 15-day experiment, we distributed a large-scale post-questionnaire to design the expanded mobile search. The design of this questionnaire will be introduced in Section 2.3.2, because the questions are based on the results of the analysis of the mobile search context found in Section 2.2.

Data Analysis

The log data that AWARE recorded included two datasets. One is Application dataset, including: (1) ID: number of data record; (2) Timestamp: timestamp of the record; (3) Package_name: name of the APP; (4)Double_end_timestamp: timestamp of the record over; and (5) Is_system_app: used to distinguish between system applications and non-system applications. The other is Keyboard dataset, including: (1) ID: the unique number of each record; (2) Timestamp: the time of keyboard input; (3) Package_name: the name of app used; (4) Current_text: the content of keyboard input; and (5) Is_password: whether participants input the password, using binary notation. The data sample is shown in Figure 1.3. In the interview, most participants said that they often search quickly on their smartphones, so we used a 15-minute gap to divide a search session.

	A	B	C	D	E
1	id	timestamp	package_name	current_text	is_password
2	16	1432112508	com.qihoo.appstore	[印章]	no
3	16	1432112598	com.qihoo.appstore	[篆印章]	no
4	16	1432284111	com.qihoo.appstore	[刻章]	no
5	16	1432523500	com.qihoo.appstore	[印章]	no
6	16	1432815050	com.UCMobile	[皇马ac]	no
7	16	1432892586	com.UCMobile	[2015足球]	no

Keyboard Dataset

	A	B	C	D	E
1	id	timestamp	package_name	double_end_timestamp	is_system_app
2	1	1431955259	com.tencent.mobileqq	1431962744	no
3	1	1431962741	com.tencent.mm	1431962744	no
4	1	1431962742	com.aware	1431962745	no
5	1	1431962743	com.baidu.input_mi	1431996902	no
6	1	1431962744	com.aware	1431996908	no
7	1	1431962744	com.tencent.mobileqq	1432003840	no

Application Dataset

Figure 1.3: The sample of two datasets.

We merged the two datasets automatically, relying on matching the IDs and Timestamps. The merged dataset contains both the query and the APP usage data, as shown in Figure 1.4.

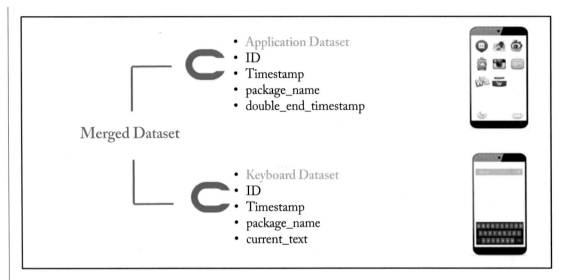

Figure 1.4: The matching method of merged dataset.

We used statistical methods to study the merged dataset such as Pointwise Mutual Information (PMI), probability statistics, ANOVA analysis, and so forth. In addition, we analyzed the contents of the questionnaire, structured diaries, and interviews, combined with certain examples to achieve the qualitative analysis for the causes.

Participants

Online questionnaires were distributed to a wide range of college students to explain our experiment and investigate mobile-search frequency in their everyday lives, the number and type of APPs installed on their mobile phones, and their level of mobile search ability. We used these questionnaires to analyze the background information of possible participants. We decided to select skilled users to participate in our experiment for two reasons: (1) we needed more mobile search records to do log analysis; and (2) experienced users were typical, and had much to say about mobile search behaviors. Participants were identified among the finalists of the 2017 "Baidu Infinite" National College Information Search Competition, hosted by Baidu. Electronic questionnaires were sent to their e-mails, and 58 students replied. We recruited 30 participants among these respondents from all over China.

The participants were all college students (9 males and 21 females), including 21 undergraduates and 9 postgraduates with an average age of 21. They came from seven universities with a variety of disciplinary backgrounds such as computer science, information science, library science, linguistics, finance, economics, psychology, and surveying and mapping.

1.4.2   USER EXPERIMENT ON CROSS-DEVICE SEARCH (EXPERIMENT II)

Experiment Settings

As found in cross-session search studies (Wang, Y. et al., 2013), users tend to resume their task with repeated searches when the task is interrupted. During cross-device search, the interval of device transition can be considered an interruption. With this in mind, we designed a user experiment with cross-device search tasks. The direction of device transition was preset and an interval was used to interrupt the task artificially, which inspired users to repeat the search.

The user experiment was conducted in a controlled laboratory environment. The cross-device search that we discussed focuses on the transition between desktop and mobile devices. Therefore, two transitions, desktop-to-mobile and mobile-to-desktop, were included in the experiment. We provided a laptop in the experiment and users were expected to use their own smartphones for the mobile search.

Cross-device Access and Fusion Engine (CAFE) (http://crosssearch.whu.edu.cn), a self-developed search system, was used to conduct the desktop and mobile search. Similar to the cross-device search system developed by Han et al. (2015a), a context-sensitive retrieval model is adopted in CAFE. The system provides users with search results by re-ranking Bing's results based on context information of MTI and viewing time. In addition, the system can remind users of previously clicked URLs by showing information about the previous device, search time, and queries.

Cross-device Search Tasks

Complex information needs cannot be satisfied by a single session and device, which makes complex information search common in cross-device search. Thus, we considered complex search tasks in the experiment. Since the task type and subtask amount affect the complexity degree of a task (Liu and Li, 2012), we designed four informational search tasks with four subtasks each in the experiment. To determine the task topics, we inquired about frequently searched topics across devices in everyday life in the participant recruitment survey. Details of the survey will be explained in Participants. We selected the top four answers as the topics of four tasks, which were Movie, Drama, Music, and Language. In order to be sure every task could not be fulfilled by a few queries in a single session, we did a pilot search of the four tasks. The result of the pilot search showed the tasks were too complex to be completed in a single session.

Four search tasks are shown in Figure 1.5. Users were provided with printed tasks, avoiding the potential problem where viewing the task on a screen influences behavior data collection. In the description of each task, four subtasks were written in bold and several instructions were given in italics. The instructions were designed to help users generate clear information needs. Users were asked to submit a report for each task, including information that was useful for the instructions.

Task Number 1
Imagine you have seen the movie *Leon* in class and you are told to write an essay about the **photography** and **lines** of the movie (*collect related information for the essay*). After class, you want to review **fragments of the movie** (*describe the content of a fragment*). Social media comments that the actress in the leading role is an outstanding person and you want to know **the reasons** (*list at least 5 reasons*).
Task Number 2
Imagine you are a fan of *House of Cards* and its Season 5 is coming back. Your memory of the **plot of Season 4** is a blur and you want to remember it (*describe the plot of Season 4*). On the day of the president's inauguration, **the trailer of Season 5** is released and you want to watch it (*describe the content of the trailer*). Discussion of Season 5 is heated on SNS and you want to know **what will be going on in Season 5** (*list at least 4 points*). You hear about two **new characters** in Season 5 and you want to know about them (*introduce the players of new characters*).
Task Number 3
Imagine you are a participant in a research group studying emoticons and you are asked to make a presentation (*collect related information for the presentation*). To begin with, you want to know **how the emoticon developed**. Then, you want to find the **differences in emoticons used by Asian and European/American people**. Last, you want to reach a conclusion about the **cultural value of emoticons**. You want to edit a message with emoticons, so you need to know **how to input emoticons on a mobile phone** (*edit a message by the way you search*).
Task Number 4
Imagine you are a fan of pop music and you want to listen to the music of the latest Billboard Hot 100 list. You like one of the songs very much and want to read its lyrics (*select a song you like and write its lyrics*). Then, you want to watch the **music video of the song ranking #27** (*describe the story of the music video*). It is well known that European and American pop music is very influential. You want to know the **influential aspects** (*list at least 4 aspects*) and the **reason they are influential** (*list at least 4 reasons*).

Figure 1.5: Cross-device search tasks (subtasks in bold, instuctions in italic).

In addition, the orders of the tasks were rotated based on task number using Latin squares to eliminate the influence of task sequence on search behavior (seen in Figure 1.6). While the sequence of device transition direction was kept fixed, the same search task was performed on different devices by different users. For example, Task 1 was searched by User 1 via desktop first and then mobile, and by User 10 via mobile first and then desktop.

Participants

Participants were recruited among university students. Electronic questionnaires were sent to students via e-mail to investigate their backgrounds and cross-search experience (see questions in Figure 1.7). The fourth survey question helped to determine the topics of the experiment tasks, and the last question helps to confirm that the participant's cross-device experience was authentic. Forty-seven people replied and were willing to participate. We recruited the 36 participants who were not familiar with the task topics of our experiment. Even though the pilot search of the four tasks showed it was difficult to complete each in one session, there were two participants who claimed that they finished the task within one session and, thus, did not search across different devices; therefore, their data was excluded. Finally, we collected the cross-device search behavior data of 34 participants (22 females and 12 males), among which there were 18 undergraduates and 16 post-graduates from 22 different majors. A third of the participants self-estimated their search ability as higher than 4 and their cross-device search frequency as higher than 3 (based on the 5-level Likert scale). We reached an agreement on privacy protection with all participants and we paid them un-equally from 100–150 yuan to encourage their serious participation (the better the performance or the more search data, the more they received).

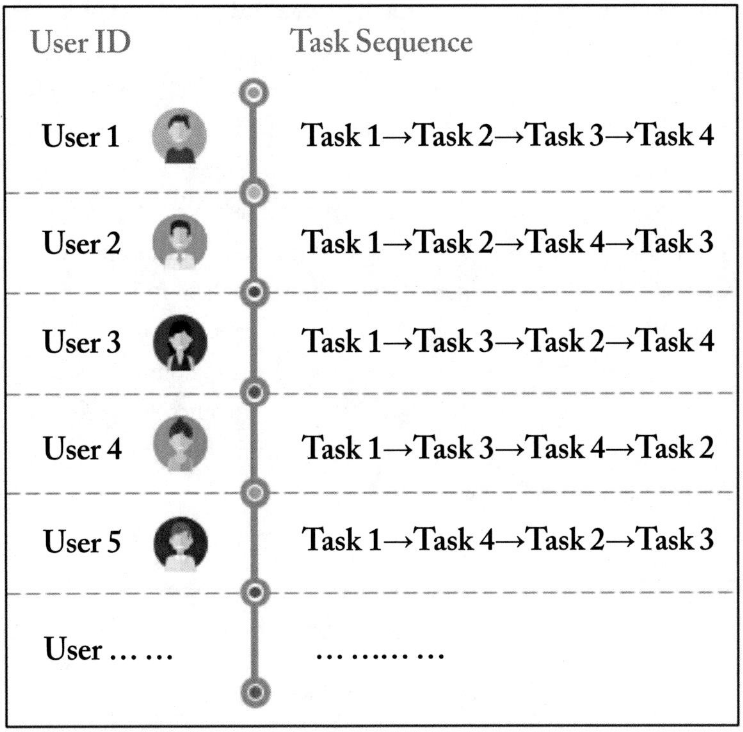

Figure 1.6: Sequence of tasks.

Participant Recruitment Survey
1. Background including sex, major, and graduation degree.
2. How good do you think your search ability is? (*5-level Likert scale*)
3. How ofter do you conduct cross-device search in daily life? (*5-level Likert scale*)
4. What are the topics you search across devices frequently? (*Multi-choice question*)
5. Describe the latest experience of cross-device search.

Figure 1.7: Questions of the participant recruitment survey.

Experiment Procedure

For each task, both desktop and mobile devices were used and participants were allowed to spend, at most, 20 min on each device. A task's search sessions were divided based on devices; therefore, every task consisted of two sessions. In order to stimulate the interruption of cross-device search activity in a real context, we designed an interval between two sessions of a task to artificially interrupt the search. We required users to complete the first session (Session 1) of each of four tasks, and then the second session (Session 2). Users were allowed to rest for 20 min after finishing Session 1 of all four tasks in order to prevent fatigue from influencing search behavior. Therefore, the intervals between two sessions of a task totaled 80 min. During the 20-min sessions, users needed not only to search for information, but also to conduct the relevance judgment and fill in the questionnaire.

We take User 1 as an example to explain the entire procedure, as seen in Figure 1.8. The procedure consisted of three stages. At the training stage, we asked User 1 to try the CAFE system and explained the entire procedure. We also told User 1 his/her task order was Task 1 → Task 2 → Task 3 → Task 4, and corresponding device transition directions. At the search stage, User 1 searched Task 1 on a desktop, Task 2 on a mobile device, Task 3 on a desktop, and Task 4 on a mobile device. During the search, User 1 was required to make a relevance judgment every time he/she clicked on a result. In addition, when User 1 claimed he/she finished the task or when the 20 min was over, he/she had to stop searching and fill in a questionnaire. Then, User 1 was asked to take a break for 20 min. After that, User 1 resumed Task 1 on a mobile device, Task 2 on a desktop, Task 3 on a mobile device, and Task 4 on a desktop, in sequence. The relevance judgment and questionnaire were conducted in the same way as above. In the final stage, we interviewed User 1 in order to better understand his behavior.

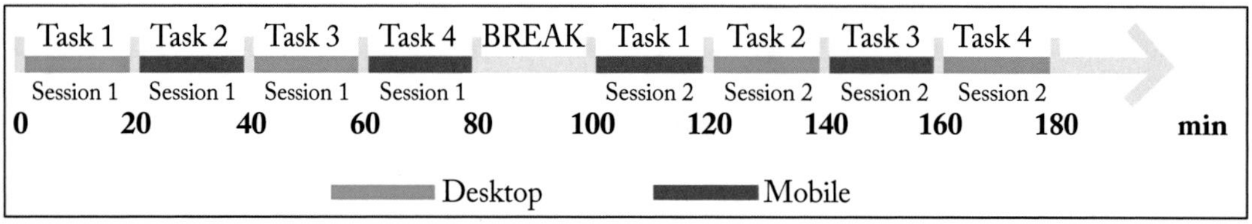

Figure 1.8: Searching stage: an example of User 1.

Over the entire procedure, every participant searched four tasks and eight sessions. In total, we collected the search behavior data of 272 sessions from 34 participants.

Data Collection

(i) CAFE System Log

The search system of both desktop and mobile search was CAFE System, the search engine result page (SERP) of which can be seen in Figures 1.9 and 1.10. Different areas of the SERP are labeled.

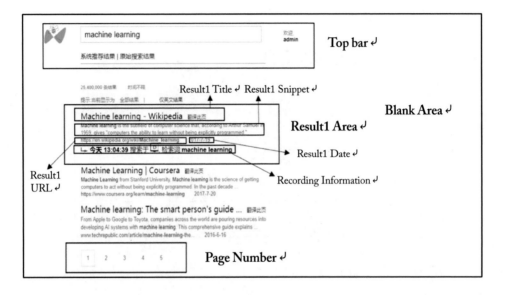

Figure 1.9: SERP of CAFE system on desktop.

The CAFE system can log SERP load time, SERP URL (including coded queries), search device, interaction types, timestamps of when the interaction started and stopped, and the areas of interactions. Desktop interactions refer to mouse movement, including move, dwell, and click, while the MTIs include drag up/down/left/right, tap and press. An example is shown in Figure 1.11. Participants issued 1,517 queries and clicked/tapped 4,069 times in total.

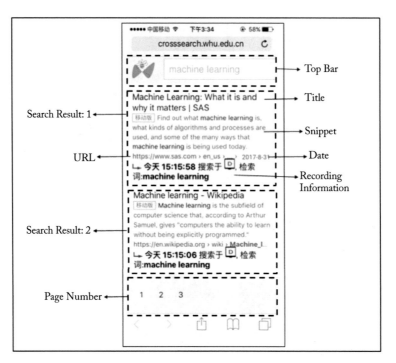

Figure 1.10: SERP of CAFE system on mobile.

username	loadtime	currenttimestamp	pageUrl	eventType	startTime	stopTime	Area	platform
admin02	1496649523964	1496649527420	http://www.bing.com/search?&q=%E7%BA%B8%E7%89%8C%E5%B1%8B%E7%AC%AC%E5%9B%9B%E5%AD%A3&first=0	dwell	1496649525644	1496649527420		Desktop
admin02	1496649523964	1496649551819	http://www.bing.com/search?&q=%E7%BA%B8%E7%89%8C%E5%B1%8B%E7%AC%AC%E5%9B%9B%E5%AD%A3&first=0	click			result2 title	Desktop

Figure 1.11: An example of system logs.

(ii) Relevance Judgment

We collected the relevance judgment of every click to analyze clicking behavior of the cross-device search on SERP. Each time participants clicked on a result, they recorded the relevance results of every judgment on paper. Information of the record can be seen in Figure 1.12. In total, the relevance judgments of 1,062 clicks were recorded. This number is less than the click/tap times recorded by the CAFE system, because the relevance judgment is only about clicking the result, while the CAFE system logs the clicks of all the areas.

```
┌──────────────────────────────────────────────────────────┐
│              Relevance Judgment Records                    │
│  1. User ID and task number                                │
│  2. Current query and device                               │
│  3. Ranking of the result you clicked                      │
│  4. Relevance of the result you clicked (5-level Likert scale)│
└──────────────────────────────────────────────────────────┘
```

Figure 1.12: Record information of the relevance judgment.

(iii) Questionnaire

In order to know whether the participant repeated a search, we used the questionnaire from Session 1 and Session 2 to record the subtasks that the participant searched. We also asked about the participant's subjective evaluation of the search task in order to understand the influence of previous devices and the search experience on the current searches, as well as to analyze the user's search performance in the cross-device search. The outline of these questionnaires is shown in Figure 1.13. In total, 272 questionnaires were collected.

```
┌──────────────────────────────────────────────────────────────────────────┐
│                      Questionnaire of Session 1                             │
│  1. User ID and task number                                                 │
│  2. What subtasks did you search (multi-level question)                     │
│  3. How familiar do you feel with each subtask? (5-level Likert scale)      │
│  4. How satisfied do you feel about the current session? (5-level Likert scale)│
│                      Questionnaire of Session 2                             │
│  1. User ID and task number                                                 │
│  2. What subtasks did you search (multi-level question)                     │
│  3. How familiar do you feel with each subtask? (5-level Likert scale)      │
│  4. How satisfied do you feel about the current session? (5-level Likert scale)│
│  5. How much does the search experience of Session 1 affect your confident/relevance judgment/structuring the │
│     query in Session 2? (5-level Likert scale)                              │
└──────────────────────────────────────────────────────────────────────────┘
```

Figure 1.13: The outline of questionnaires in the experiment.

(iv) Interview

The outline of the interview is shown in Figure 1.14. These questions were designed with regard to the questionnaire of Session 1 and Session 2 in order to understand the reasons behind performing cross-device searches. Sound recordings of 34 participants were saved.

Interview Outline

1. What did you search—(*subtask*) on desktop and —(*subtask*) on mobile? (*corresponding to the second question of Questionnaire of Session 1 and Session 2*)
2. Why the familiarity with—(*subtask*) became more/less? (*corresponding to the third question of Questionnaire of Session 1 and Session 2*)
3. Why did you feel less satisfied with Session X (*corresponding to the fourth question of Questionnaire of Session 2*)
4. Explain how the experience of Session 1 affected your search behavior in Session 2. (*corresponding to the fifth question of Questionnaire of Session 2*)

Figure 1.14: The outline of interview.

Data Analysis

With data from the CAFE system logs, we used the ID and Timestamp to differentiate the unique users. We used several methods to analyze the data collected from different aspects. We used machine learning to model the user's cross-device search behavior and to analyze the importance of the feature in prediction, such as Binary Logistic Regression (BLR), C5.0 Decision Tree (C5.0), and Support Vector Machine (SVM).

As for the analysis of cross-device search performance, we evaluated users' search performance through the calculation of search accuracy, effective search time, nDCG, p@n (precision of top n results), and satisfaction. The data from the questionnaire was analyzed by several statistical analysis methods. The content of users' interviews supports the analysis of influencing factors on search performance.

CHAPTER 2

Context-based Mobile Search Behaviors

In this chapter, we study users' mobile search strategies from the perspectives of mobile search information needs and motivations, mobile search query formulation, mobile search query reformulation, and various mobile search contexts. This section mainly addresses user Experiment I.

2.1 MOBILE SEARCH STRATEGIES

As an important aspect of users' behavior, mobile users' search strategies play an important role in understanding users' search intentions and search behavior characteristics. We intend to study users' behavior through in-depth analysis of their information needs within a search session context, combined with examining the recorded search logs, which contain detailed user behavior on querying, selecting, and reviewing in the search sessions. Studying mobile search strategies will help to understand the features of users' search behaviors and can enable mobile service providers to better serve users' search habits and information needs. Therefore, we examined the relationship between the search session and query, characterized the features of mobile search sessions, discussed the factors of these features, and compared the behaviors of our participants to those of the populations in existing studies. Then, we detected the various context dimensions of mobile search from the users' daily mobile phone usages, which contributed to the conduct of the multi-dimensional model of mobile search behavior.

2.1.1 MOBILE SEARCH INFORMATION NEEDS AND MOTIVATIONS

Mobile Search Information Need

Users' search content is an important aspect of the research on mobile search. In their daily searches, users are accustomed to using uncontrolled words (natural language) with a wide topic distribution, which is not conducive to topic classification of search content.

In Experiment I, we defined the "Query" as complete text content entered by the user during the search process and marked it as Qi (i = 1,2 . . .). The "current_text" in the data set from AWARE indicates the user's queries. In this experiment, a total of 2,875 queries submitted by 30 users within 2 weeks were collected. "Query length" represents the number of Chinese characters or English words, collectively called characters. "Query length" was marked as Lq ($Lq \geq 1$).

In total, participants submitted 2,875 queries during the experiment. There are different criteria to identify the search session, such as time, IP address, and cookie (He et al., 2002; Eickhoff et al., 2014). In the interview, most participants said they often searched quickly on smartphones, so we used a 15-min gap to divide a search session, meaning that a search session ended if there were no more queries for 15 min or longer. There were 1,781 search sessions in this experiment, and we marked the search session as Si (i = 1, 2,...). At the same time, "search session length" represents the number of queries contained in a search session, and was marked as Ls($Ls \geq 1$).

We mapped all queries submitted by users to controlled words or their hypernyms in the "Chinese Classified Thesaurus" (http://cct.nlc.cn/login.aspx), a popular classification theme in China. The replacement rule is as follows. (1) If the original query is a controlled word that can be accurately mapped to the "Chinese Classified Thesaurus," it can be directly replaced by a standard controlled word, and the mapping category is marked as "accurate." (2) As the "Chinese Classified Thesaurus" is a classification of vocabulary, not all words belonging to a certain category can be mapped. In terms of those queries that could not be accurately mapped, they are mapped instead to standard words in the high-level category in the "Chinese Classified Thesaurus" according to the original query semantics. For instance, "Where Are We Going, Dad?" (a variety show) should be replaced with "TV show." The mapping category is labeled as "upper class." (3) Special nouns require special handling, including professional terms for disciplines, people's names, geographical names, song titles, and network-based language. The original query should be uniformly processed by using conventional alternative words for retainment and the mapping category is consistent with the corresponding category the special noun belongs to. (4) Language translation processing consists of translation from English to Chinese and from Chinese to English. With regard to the former, the original English query should be replaced by "word" and "phrase." As for the latter, the original query should be replaced with "Chinese character" and "word" according to the Chinese structure. The mapping category of translation from English to Chinese is marked as "query translation," and the mapping category of translation from Chinese to English is marked as "translation query." (5) For semantically unknown and unrecognized queries, like when a single word or letter are concerned, we adopt a completely reserved method. This mapping category is marked as "noise point."

Figure 2.1 shows the statistical analysis of queries that have been replaced by controlled words by means of visual processing; in order to allow fuller understanding, we replaced the controlled words with English in Figures 2.1 and 2.2.

The larger the font, the higher frequency of the query. In Figure 2.1, distribution of large fonts is apparent, reflecting a concentrated distribution of users' query content. For example, "word" and "translation" are bigger than the other words, reflecting the popularity of their searches. These words in particular are common because the participants of Experiment I are college students who have a relatively greater need to translate a foreign language. Additionally, "APP," "TV," "song," "movie," and "restaurant" account for high proportions as well, denoting the college students' need for recreational and lifestyle information. Moreover, smaller fonts are abundant and dispersedly distributed. In order to better show query topic distribution, we used subject indexing for queries that have been replaced by controlled words.

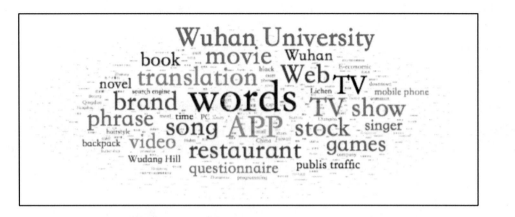

Figure 2.1: Query distribution after replacement with controlled words.

Researchers use different classification criteria in view of query content in users' search logs (Komaki et al., 2012; Sohn et al., 2010; Hinze et al., 2010). In this chapter, we used an open classification directory, DMOZ (http: //www.dmoz.org), to analyze the query topic distribution. All queries could be divided into 14 topics, as seen in Figure 2.2.

Figure 2.2: Topic distribution of queries.

User-submitted queries in this experiment could primarily be classified into five types: "reference," "arts," "shopping," "computers," and "science." Having specifically analyzed these queries according to second-level directories of DMOZ's open classification directory, we found that searches for "reference" information mainly involved searches for map, dictionary, and encyclopedia information. Information needs for "arts" were mainly concentrated in the fields of music, videos, and literary works. Searches for "shopping" information focused on food, beauty products, and consumer electronics. For "computer" information, users mainly searched for various mobile APPs. Searches for "science" information were mainly concentrated in the fields of social science and natural science, such as chemistry, computer science, earth science, history, and so on. As our participants were all college students from different subjects, we divided the searches for "science" into "natural science" and "social science" in the following analysis. These 14 topics reflect the users' different information needs as noted in Table 2.1.

Table 2.1: Categories of information need types	
Category	Examples
Reference	English-French translation: Where is post office?
Shopping	iPad, Lipstick, Handbag male
Arts	Batman movie, Gone with the Wind,
Computers	Python, Machine learning
Science	History of New Zealand, E-commerce
Society	Famous people in Hubei
Recreation	Wudang Hill travel, Happy Valley
News	Shipwreck accident, UN General Assembly
Business	Apple stock code, Financial products
Games	GTA5, Angry Birds
Health	Toothache, How to ease the headache?
Sports	Real Madrid, NFL
Region	Wuhan, Chicago
Kids and teens	Children's Day, Children's books recommendations

Mobile Search Motivation

Participants were asked to use structured diaries to record which motivations defined their most memorable search sessions each day. In the last section, we classified information needs by analyzing all query topics; additionally, we identified 450 mobile search sessions with definite information needs from the structured diaries. We found that users were commonly driven by multiple motivations to finish one mobile search session. We defined six motivation categories in our research to meet every search session.

1. *Curiosity* is a category that reflects the user's interest in an unfamiliar topic that occurs by chance, e.g., while watching a movie and wanting more details about an actor or while chatting with a friend and wanting to prove a point.

2. *Time killing* is a category that refers to the desire for recreation in one's spare time, where the desired information is useless but recreational, e.g., looking for amusing news or information about celebrities.

3. *Knowledge* is a category that refers to needs derived from the user's profession, e.g., an IT student searching for information about a programming language.

4. *Life service* includes needs arising in daily life, such as finding directions to a location.

5. Social relations includes two types of searches: seeking contact information for a company with regard to employment information; and false searches, done to appear busy in order to avoid developing a relationship or chatting with somebody in social situations.

6. *Others* includes motivations that do not fall into any of the above categories.

Table 2.2 is a matrix of participants' information-seeking motivations. It illustrates searches with one or two motivations. For searches with more than two motivations, we add one for each pair of motivations in that particular search. For example, one participant chose time killing, curiosity, and social relations as the motivations for a mobile search session. We added one to the frequency for each of the following: the relationship between curiosity and social relations, the relationship between time killing and curiosity, and the relationship between time killing and social relations. After all the integers of frequency were added, we calculated the percentages of information-seeking motivations by the equation below. IntRre is the number of searches driven by a particular motivation):

$$\text{Percentage} = \frac{IntRre}{450} \; .$$

Integers in Table 2.2 refer to the frequency of search sessions stemming from the motivation in the column. Percentages refer to the ratio of search sessions driven by a certain motivation to total search sessions.

Table 2.2: Matrix of search motivations							
Information	Curiosity	Time Killing	Knowledge	Life Service	Social Relations	Others	Total
Curiosity	79 (17.56%)	38	39	14	3	4	177
Time Killing	8.44%	31(6.89%)	22	8	2	5	106
Knowledge	8.67%	4.89%	88(19.56%)	16	1	7	173
Life Service	3.11%	1.78%	3.56%	95 (21.11%)	-	6	137
Social Relations	0.67%	0.44%	0.22%	-	10(2.22%)	1	17
Others	0.89%	1.11%	1.56%	1.33%	0.22%	19(4.22%)	40
Total	39.33%	23.56%	38.44%	30.44%	3.78%	8.89%	650 (144.00%)

Results show that 71.56% of all mobile search sessions originate from a single search motivation, and 24.44% originate from two search motivations. The remaining 4% stem from three search motivations. Mobile search sessions are mainly motivated by curiosity and knowledge, which account for 77.78% of the total. Search sessions motivated by daily life services and time killing are the second largest group. Even though there is a low rate of searches driven by building or avoiding social relations, we concluded that participants are driven by relatively balanced motivations to perform mobile searches in their daily life, and they rely on mobile search to meet various information needs.

On the other hand, mobile search sessions overall are driven by an average of 1.44 types of motivations. Search sessions driven by curiosity, time killing, and knowledge share high rates of correlation. More specifically, time-killing searches are prone to be influenced by other motivations, such as curiosity and knowledge. Search sessions for life services are relatively independent of the others.

Relationship between Mobile Search Motivation and Information Need

As mentioned above, we classified the queries into 14 topics, according to the DMOZ. In this section, we analyzed motivation and information need types via cross tabulation and found significant correlations between them, shown in Table 2.3.

Table 2.3: Mobile search motivation and information need

Motivation	Correlations (p-value)
Curiosity	0.038*
Time-killing	0.118
Knowledge	0.020*
Life service	0.000**
Social relations	0.358
Social avoidance	0.910
Others	0.354
Note: ** p<0.01, * p<0.05.	

We also analyzed three significant motivation correlations to understand the information need types under different motivations, as shown in Table 2.4.

Table 2.4: Top three relationships between search motivation and information need type

Motivation	Top 1 (%)	Top 2 (%)	Top 3 (%)
Curiosity	Arts (31.1)	Social science (22.2)	Recreation (6.7)
Knowledge	Arts (22.4)	Social science (16.1)	Computers (12.6)
Life service	Arts (18.0)	Recreation (15.6)	Shopping (12.5)
Note: Percentage referred to the ratio of certain information need to all mobile searches.			

Tables 2.3 and 2.4 indicate that three types of motivations have significant correlations with information need. Driven by various search motivations, participants appear to have diverse information needs. We conclude that college students' need for arts information was commonly higher than for other information types. When participants searched to satisfy their curiosity, their need for social sciences and recreation information were relatively higher. When they searched to increase their knowledge, their need for social sciences and computer information were also relatively higher. When participants decided to search to satisfy daily life needs, they tended to find information on recreation and shopping.

2.1.2   MOBILE SEARCH QUERY FORMULATION

Query Language

Among all mobile search queries, Chinese language queries (2,205) account for 76.7%, followed by English language queries (19.93%) and Chinese-English mixed queries (3.37%). The proportions of both English-language queries and Chinese-English mixed queries in our study are higher than the results of J. Wang et al. (2013) (2.26%, and less than 2.77%, respectively), suggesting that an English environment has a great impact on college students.

It is natural for our participants to use Chinese-language queries for mobile searches in a Chinese environment. We found that 70.82% of the English-language queries stem from the translation of English words or phrases. Other English-language queries involve stock code, English brands (e.g., airline number, APP name), as well as English nouns without the corresponding translation in Chinese and their abbreviations.

Chinese-English mixed queries mainly come from a combination of English-language brands and product model numbers used in daily life, such as digital product model numbers (MX4 Pro, iPad Air, Win7), social APPs (QQ, zaka, Facebook), foreign language (DIY, COS), computer language (DSN, Python), and so on. This reflects the fact that foreign vocabulary has an important influence on participants' lives in the Chinese-language environment. Table 2.5 shows the source of English words in English-language queries and Chinese-English-language mixed queries.

Table 2.5: Source of English words in queries

Source of Queries in English language		Number	Percentage (%)	Example
Translation	Word	384	60.57	compact
	Phrase	65	10.25	call upon
Stock code		26	4.1	nmhd
English brand in Chinese environment		58	9.15	MX4/MIUI/ TCL
English proper noun and its abbreviation		48	7.57	Coursera/GIS
Computer language and corresponding abbreviation		16	2.52	javascript/DCL
URL		10	1.58	www.baidu.com

Time and Input Duration of Query Formulation

The analysis of the submission times of all queries indicates that they are widely distributed in the daytime, and mobile searches are more active in this period. Additionally, their mobile search behaviors are more frequent in the afternoon and at night than in the morning, as shown in Figure 2.3. The peak time for queries in daily life is consistent with the results of J. Wang et al. (2013), obtained from log analysis of a large academic website. In our study, there are two obvious peaks at 15:00 and 20:00.

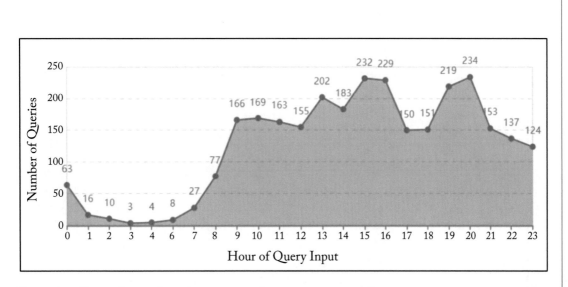

Figure 2.3: Time of query formulation in one day.

Among all mobile search queries, 89.22% were submitted within 10 s. The queries submitted within 2 seconds account for the most, and the average input duration is 4.75 s. In addition, the input duration of Chinese-language queries is 4.21 s on average, and English-language queries is 5.6 s on average, while the input duration of Chinese-English mixed queries is 11.92 s on average. This indicates that Chinese-English inputs are the most time consuming.

Taking into account the effects of language and query length on query input duration (as shown in Figure 2.4), we find that there is a clear and stable linear correlation between Chinese-language query input duration and query length, and there is a fluctuant correlation between English-language query input duration and query length. However, the correlation between Chinese-English mixed query input duration and query length is not obvious. When the query length is no more than four characters, the input duration of Chinese-language queries is shorter than that of English-language queries. Furthermore, if the query length is over four, the input duration of Chinese-language queries is longer than that of English-language queries with the same query length.

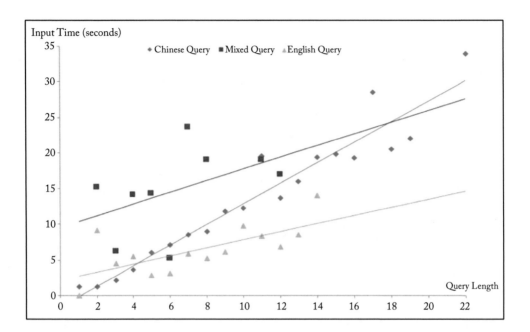

Figure 2.4: Relationship between query length and input duration of multilingual query.

Length and Structure of Query

Regardless of the language of a query, the mean query length is 2.59 characters. The longest query contains 22 Chinese characters: "if a transaction fails, the update which has been done will be restored" (translated from Chinese into English). The shortest query contains just one character, such as a word or a letter. The average query length in this study is within the range of previous studies (2.1–2.7 characters), with a slight increase (Church et al., 2008).

The distribution of different query lengths is shown in Figure 2.5: the query $1 \leq Lq \leq 4$ accounts for 75.05%, and the query with two characters accounts for the highest proportion. This is closely associated with Chinese vocabulary structure, as a Chinese query always appears as a single term containing two words. Most of the queries with one character are English-language queries, and most queries with three characters are Chinese-English mixed queries, mainly appearing in the form of one English word with two Chinese characters.

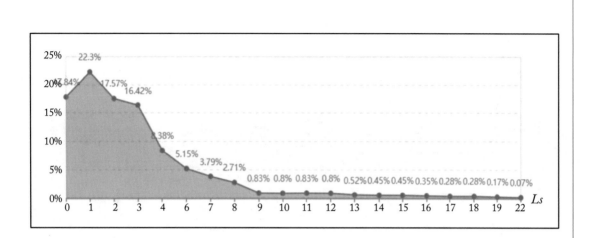

Figure 2.5: Proportions of mobile search query lengths.

Having segmented a query into single Chinese characters, English words, single terms, strings, and sentences, we can see that single Chinese characters/English words, strings, and sentences account for similar proportions of 18%, 11%, and 14%, respectively. A vast majority of queries (57%) are single words. The structure features of queries are consistent with length features. Overall, the structure of mobile search queries is diverse and clear—consistent with what Church et al. (2008) found—while the rangeability of query length in this study is smaller, and the number of long length queries is higher.

Number of Average Search Sessions and Queries

Church et al. (2007) studied European mobile users' search behaviors, finding that each user submitted an average of 1.5 search sessions per day. Another study (Church and Smyth, 2008a) also found that more than 50% of users only submitted one query.

However, in this experiment, there are 4.24 search sessions per day, and users submitted an average of 6.85 queries per day. This may because our participants, recruited from those with a great deal of search experience, prefer searching on mobile devices. Results about average number of search sessions and queries per user per day can be seen in Figure 2.6.

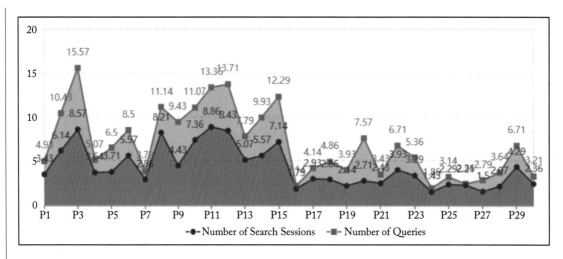

Figure 2.6: Average number of search sessions and queries per user per day.

In this study, users with more than 2 search sessions per day account for 90% of the results, and half of the users submitted more than 6 queries per day on average. Specifically, the number of search sessions of participants *P3*, *P8*, *P10*, *P11*, and *P15* is more than 7 on average, and these users submitted more than 10 queries per day. Combining the background information in the questionnaire for analysis, we find that these five participants primarily major in library and information science, information management, and information system, thereby possessing high information literacy.

In addition, the number of search sessions and queries per day of our participants are both greater than typical mobile searchers in other studies (Church et al., 2007, 2008). This indicates that college students may have more abundant daily information needs and use mobile phones to search for information more frequently. All of the participants in this experiment were contestants of the semifinal of 2015 "Baidu Infinite" National College Information Search Competition, which indicates their proficient search ability and higher frequency of mobile search.

Length of Search Session

When users search on mobile phones, they often satisfy their information needs through simple interactions. Jansen et al. (2006) did not merely segment search sessions according to IP addresses and cookies in search logs. Instead, they combined time with users' search content to determine search sessions. They found that over 90% of search sessions consist of three or fewer queries. The survey of 2.6 million European mobile users carried out by Church et al. (2008) found that nearly 60% of mobile search sessions consist of only a single query. Vojnovic et al. (2008) came to similar conclusions, finding that 61.87% of mobile search sessions contain only one query.

Our study divides 2,875 queries into 1,781 search sessions. The mean search session length is 1.61 queries and 69.06% of the search sessions consist of one query, which presents an upward trend of proportion compared with previous research (Jansen et al., 2006; Church et al., 2008; Vojnovic et al., 2008). It is becoming more and more common for users to end search activities with a single query when they use mobile phones. This also reflects continuous improvement in users' searching abilities. In addition, search sessions with two or more queries still account for a high proportion (30.94%). The proportion of search sessions with more than 3 queries is 13.53%, which is also higher than that of Jansen et al. (2006).

2.1.3   MOBILE SEARCH QUERY REFORMULATION

Query Reformulation in Search Session

In Experiment I, there were 399 query reformulations in 237 search sessions. We analyzed the statistical results of query reformulation in search sessions and queries, as shown in Table 2.6. In the search session, the minimum reformulation frequency is 1 and the maximum reformulation frequency is 5.

Table 2.6: Statics of reformulations in search sessions and queries

	Search Sessions	Queries
At least one reformulation	237 (13.31%)	399 (13.88%)
No reformulation	1,544 (86.67%)	2,476 (86.12%)
One reformulation	198 (83.54%)	332 (83.21%)
Average of reformulation	2.01	1.19

Fewer query reformulation behaviors and lower mean reformulation frequency in this experiment suggest that query reformulation in mobile search demonstrates a decreasing trend. This is partly because query input is more accurate and convenient through a mobile phone, and the search engine has gained optimization to identify fuzzy queries.

We also investigated mobile search query reformulation patterns and divided these reformulations into two types: error correction and adjustment reformulation, the results of which are shown in Table 2.7. Correction for typo-type errors (wrong word/Chinese character) is the main type of query reformulation (31.59%), followed by correction for homophone errors (22.02%), and correction for wrong pinyin coming from the same keyboard input (18.13%). As for adjustment reformulations, users mainly reformulated queries by adding or reducing the qualifier to narrow or expand retrieval range.

Table 2.7: Method of query reformulation

Reformulation Pattern	Reformulation Method	Percentage (%)	Query Before Reformulation	Query After Reformulation
Error correction	Correct type errors	31.59	*Moderater*	*moderator*
	Delete auto-filled query and re-enter query	4.77	*Fcbarcelona*	*fcbanking*
	Correct homophone errors	22.02	*Father*	*farther*
	Correct wrong query coming from same keyboard input	18.13	*Andy*	*Body*
	Correct synonymy, quasi-homonymy errors	2.73	*restaurant*	*luncheonette*
	Correct operator errors	3.57	*Running! man*	*Running man*
Adjustment reformulation	Add qualifier	2.30	*hotel*	*Wudang hotel*
	Delete qualifier	6.12	*lose weight in a healthy way*	*lose weight*
	Without change reformulation	3.76	*steamed vermicelli roll*	*steamed vermicelli roll*
	Input query—search engine—input reformulation	3.27	*Wuhan—Google—Wuhan University Library*	
	Switch-over between full name and abbreviated name, English and Chinese, uppercase and lowercase	1.74	*HBM*	*Health Behavior Model*

Note: (1) Reformulation without change means that the user entered the same query after the first query. (2) Input—search engine—input reformulation means that the user first enters in the default search box after opening a browser and then comes to a homepage of a search engine to continue the last search.

Situations with incorrect query input vary. Users' operational mistakes may cause errors in query input. For example, users may type the wrong query even if they had known what they meant to input. Since many search engines have realized query recommendation and query autofill based on user context, the user could manually delete incorrect queries and re-enter them when the recommendation and query autofill was far from what users needed. Additionally, users may incorrectly choose a query coming from the same keyboard input when they used the nine-key pinyin input method (in a Chinese language input environment).

Pattern of Queries Change in Search Session

When searching for information on mobile phones, users sometimes need to input more queries to meet their information needs. Moreover, in a unique search session, users might continue modifying queries based on search results in order to complete search tasks.

He et al. (2002) defined the reformulation in search sessions, which is a kind of search pattern. If two consecutive activities in one search session are about the same topic, the difference between the queries could be regarded as reformulation. Jansen et al. (2006) classified queries in one search session into initial query (first one submitted by a user) and subsequent query (submitted after the initial query). They also defined query classifications as follows: generalization, hierarchical, parallel, reformulation, and specialization. Church et al. (2007) classified queries in the search session into four types: initial, modified, identical, and zero-term. Classifying multiple queries in the search session can describe changes in users' search strategies during the search process, changes of information need, progress of search tasks, and satisfaction of search results, which is of great significance when studying user search behaviors.

Using 551 search sessions with more than 1 query as the base, we analyzed the initial and subsequent queries in each session from several perspectives, such as content, time, and APP used, considering users' information needs, search motivations, and so on. These 551 search sessions consist of 1,645 queries (with 551 initial queries), and we classified the 1,094 subsequent queries into 3 types, as seen in Table 2.8.

Table 2.8: Pattern of subsequent query in search session

Pattern of Subsequent Query		Number of queries	Percentage (%)
Continuous search		547	50.00
Extended search	Related needs	346	31.63
	New needs	115	10.51
Repetitive search	A period of interruption	42	3.84
	Change another APP	44	4.02

Continuous search (50.00%) means that users continue to search for information by modifying the queries or keywords in detail after the initial search due to low satisfaction with the initial search results. Furthermore, continuous searches also suggest that users must satisfy their information needs within a short timeframe. For instance, participant $P5$ did not find satisfactory results after submitting the query "aphasia." He/she continued to submit two queries, "aphasia language research" and "anomic aphasia," and finished the search session. In the structured diary, participant $P5$ described this search experience as "important" and "urgent" and said that the search process was "uninterrupted."

Extended search (42.14%) is an expression about an extension of users' information needs in a search session. According to the relevance between users' search contents, we classify them into extended search triggered by related information needs and extended search triggered by new information needs.

Extended search triggered by related information needs (31.63%) refers to users who searched for information related to the topics of initial searches. For example, participant $P6$ continued to search for "ipadair2 liner (Q_{656})" and "ipadair2 protective shell (Q_{657})," after searching for "ipadair2 jacket (Q_{655})." Users submitted more queries when they searched for tourism information; for example, participant $P7$ searched for other scenic spots in Suzhou, such as "Suzhou moat (Q_{743})" and "Suzhou Restaurante Chino ($Q744$)" after searching for "Humble Administration Garden in Suzhou (Q_{742})."

Extended search triggered by new information needs always means that users searched for other information related to a new information need, unrelated to the initial query. For example, participant $P14$ submitted the query "the origin of Children's Day" after entering query "the origin of Mother's Day." There is no direct relation between the content of these two queries. Referring back to the structured diary of that day, however, participant $P14$ mentioned that he/she only wanted to search for "the origin of Mother's Day" at that time.

Repetitive search (7.86%) means that users continue to submit the same query in a search session. There are two reasons for repetitive searches. One is that, for some reason, the user resumes search tasks after an initial search is interrupted. For instance, participant $P4$ mentioned in the interview that "when I searched for whether the post office of Bayi Road was still there, the search was interrupted by discussion with friends." In another example, participant $P10$ searched for "let it be (Q_{1164})" through KuGou Music (a music APP in China). Six minutes later, he/she searched for "let it be (Q_{1165})" again. In the structured diary, user $P10$ also mentioned that the search process was interrupted. Search interruptions can be related to users' social environment. For search sessions with interruptions mentioned by users, 52.24% of them occurred when the user was "with classmates, friends, or strangers." Another reason is that users utilized another APP to submit the same query. For instance, participant $P6$ used Mobile Taobao (a shopping APP like Amazon) to search for "Polaroid (Q_{666})" at first, and used Baidu Mobile (a mobile search engine) to continue the search

"Polaroid (Q_{667})." The main reason users utilized other APPs for repetitive searches is that they had low satisfaction with the current search results or the search failed. For example, participant P1 searched for "Xiaosong Talkshow (Q_{61})" via Sohu Video (a video APP), and then he/she switched to IQIYI (another video APP) and searched it again. This is because the Sohu Video did not have the copyright of this talk show. Participant P9 used Baidu Mobile and NetEase Cloud Music (a music APP) to search for "Walk Out of Mountain Tomorrow," respectively, and he said the reason he changed APPs was that "Baidu didn't tell me which song the lyrics ware from."

2.1.4   MOBILE SEARCH SESSION ANALYSIS

Type of Search Sessions

Researchers have classified search sessions from different perspectives. Eickhoff et al. (2014) identified users' information needs from query syntax and divided search sessions into procedural and declarative sessions based on the search task. Broder (2002) classified queries into three types: navigational, informational, and transactional, according to users' search tasks and intent. Hassan et al. (2014) analyzed users' search process and divided search sessions into struggling session and exploring session. There are also some classifications about search sessions based on different types of queries (Hinze et al., 2010). Amin et al. (2009) divided search sessions into three types: (1) fact finding, which means that users search for specific factual pieces of information; (2) information gathering, which means that users constantly search for certain information to fulfill particular goals; and (3) non-goal-oriented information seeking, which means that the motivation of a search activity is to look for information users are interested in. Consulting the classification on Amin's research, Cui et al. (2008) divided search sessions into three types: fact finding, information gathering, and casual browsing..

Based on the previous studies that the classification criteria provide (Amin et al., 2009; Cui et al., 2008), and combining it with the experimental data and structured diaries, we divided all search sessions into three categories from the angles of search task and search motivation. These types and examples are shown in Table 2.9.

Table 2.9: Categories of search session

Categories	Frequency	Examples					
		User ID	Search Session ID	Query ID	Search Time	APP Name	Query Content
Gathering knowledge	516	P2	S112	Q176	10:40:40	Baidu Browser	*Chemical bonds of ozone*
		P3	S191	Q343	13:19:00	Baidu Mobile	*Maslow demand*
Goal-oriented	632	P8	S479	Q772	21:59:38	MI APP Store	*Jingdong Mall*
				Q773	22:01:21	Jingdong Mall	*Purple female*
		P12	S986	Q1563	13:11:58	MI Store	*Xiaomi mobile power*
				Q1564	13:14:35	Mobile Taobao	*Xiaomi Charger Pal*
Non-goal-oriented	633	P25	S1,594	Q2563	12:58:53	Sina Microblog	*Affectionate girl*
		P30	S1,760	Q2843	12:16:32	Opera Mini	*Ministry of Health logo*

A gathering knowledge session focuses on urgent information needs or tasks. Users are motivated to search online due to information needs or search tasks arising during study and work. Analysis of the structured diaries finds that in terms of user's mobile searches for "Gathering knowledge," 91% of search sessions were not interrupted and 82% of search sessions took place while the user was "learning." This kind of search session accounts for 28.97%, reflecting participants' great need for information related to learning or work, which is related to their identity as university student.

A goal-oriented search session refers to a search activity in which users have further management on search results after searches. For instance, a user searched for the same products on different shopping websites to compare prices, then he/she searched for APPs in the mobile application market and downloaded one. Finally, he/she booked a hotel after searching for hotel information and shared the search results via a social APP. In this kind of search session, users' search behavior mainly occurs in the early stage of the search process, existing for the fulfillment of the primary goal. In our dataset, this kind of search session accounts for 35.49%, indicating that mobile search plays a supportive role in user's learning, work, and life. For example, as shown in Table 2.9, participant *P8* first queried "Jingdong Mall," aiming to download the APP to further search for other commodities. Participant *P12* compared prices of the same products by searching in different APPs, and also mentioned in the interview that "I searched for power supply in Mi Store first to view introductions and comments, and then switched to Taobao to view commodity details."

A non-goal-oriented search session refers to search activity generated from users' personal interest or curiosity in their daily life. In non-goal-oriented search sessions, users do not have clear goals and their information needs are neither urgent nor generally important. This kind of search session accounts for the highest proportion (35.54%). According to the structured diaries, when the search was triggered by "curiosity," 76.28% of search sessions took place when user was "at rest" and 92.95% of users considered the search "not important/not urgent" or "neutral."

Time Span of Search Sessions

In order to facilitate the statistics, we selected a minute as the time unit when analyzing the time span of search session, represented by Ts (Ts ≥1 min). The mean time span of 1,781 search sessions in Experiment I was 2.32 min, among which 79.45% of search sessions were shorter than 1 min. This result is slightly lower than the results of Jansen et al. (2006). In our study, 88.55% of search sessions were shorter than 5 min, which is close to the results of Vojnovic (2008). Without consideration of the search sessions consisting of only one query, the mean time span of the 551 remaining search sessions was 5.26 min. The time span distributions are shown in Figure 2.7.

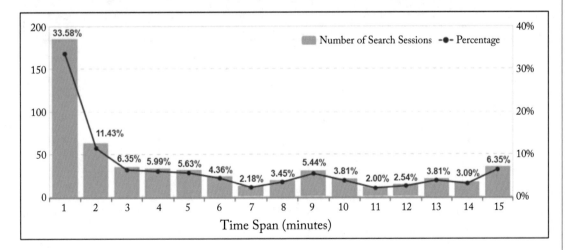

Figure 2.7: Time span of search sessions with more than one query.

Through statistical analysis, we find that the average time span of the 185 search sessions with more than 1 query was still less than 1 min, which reflects that users tend to complete a mobile search task in a short time. Moreover, analysis of the search sessions that left the deepest impression on users, according to their diary entries, finds that, when users thought "information needs in the search are important or urgent," the mean time span of the search sessions was 1.75

min. This indicates that the importance and urgency of users' information needs have an effect on the time span of the search session.

At the same time, we made a statistical analysis of the average time span of search sessions with different lengths, the results of which are shown in Figure 2.8. The statistical result finds that the average time span increases as the length of the search session grows when $Ls < 7$, and the average time span of the search session presents an irregular distribution $Ls \geq 7$. Analysis of search sessions where $Ls < 7$ finds that among these search sessions, users mainly searched for the same topics of information, such as "reference," "shopping," and "arts."

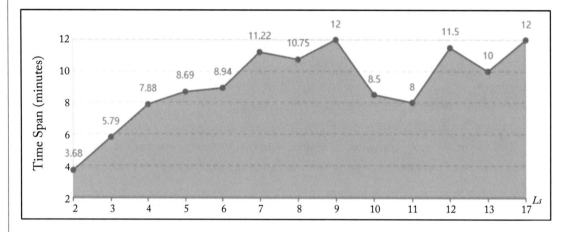

Figure 2.8: Average time span of search sessions with different lengths.

2.1.5   DETECTING VARIOUS CONTEXT DIMENTIONS OF MOBILE SEARCH

In Experiment I, we were able to collect logs of daily mobile phone use by installing AWARE, as well as through structured diaries and deep interviews after the experiment. All participants were asked to submit the structured diaries to identify the most memorable search daily. Information needs, information-seeking motivations, search sites, and contexts were requested in the structured diary, as well as any interruption of the mobile search session.

In this section, we define mobile search context as the personal attributes and surroundings of the participants when conducting a mobile search, including the physical environment (e.g., indoor, outdoor, and specific place) and the social environment (e.g., alone or with others). There are 12 defined dimensions of participants' mobile search context (Table 2.10), which can be divided into 3 categories. We obtained this information from the structured diaries and the phone logs, and did correlation analysis or difference analysis between context dimensions and mobile search behaviors. The analysis tool used was Statistical Product and Service Solutions (SPSS 19.0), and analytical methods are cross tabulation and one-way analysis of variance (ANOVA).

Table 2.10: Dimensions of participants' mobile search context

Category	Dimension	Definition	Source
Personal attributes of the participant	Gender	Sex (male or female)	Structured diary
	Age	Participant age	Interview
	Grade	Freshman, sophomore, junior or senior	Log
	Major	Academic field	Log
Physical environment of the participant	Time	Year-month-day-hour-minute-second	Log
	Place	Indoor or outdoor; specific location	Log
	Weather	Summer, rainy or sunny	Log
	Device	Phone type and screen size	Weather report
Social environment of the participant	Activity	Event involved while searching: resting, working, studying, shopping, traveling, etc.	Structured diary
	Relations	Accompanied or alone	Structured diary
	Importance	Whether the search task is urgent	Structured diary
	Portal	APP used	Log

2.2 MODELING CONTEXT-BASED MOBILE SEARCH

As the popularity of mobile search among young people continues to grow (iiMedia, 2017), many mobile service providers have ventured into mobile search APP development to attract college students. In order to design applications and services for particular information needs and mobile contexts, it is necessary to understand how mobile search context influences search behaviors, such as information need, search effectiveness, and so on. The dimensional context of mobile searches may have correlations between any two dimensions. In this section, we explore significant correlations to better understand how the mobile search context affects mobile search behaviors. The analysis results are presented in Tables 2.11 and 2.12. The "P" in Table 2.11 stands for partially correlated, i.e., a subdivision of a certain dimension correlates with another dimension or a subdivision of the dimension.

Table 2.11: Personal attributes and physical environment

Context		Personal attributes (p-value)				Natural environments (p-value)			
		Gender	Age	Grade	Major	Time	Place	Weather	Device
Personal attributes	Gender	—	—	—	—	0.673	P	—	—
	Age	—	—	—	—	0.347	0.748	—	—
	Grade	—	—	—	—	0.284	0.345	—	—
	Major	—	—	—	—	0.529	0.653	—	—
Natural environments	Time	0.673	0.347	0.284	0.529	—	0.354	0.736	—
	Place	P	0.748	0.345	0.653	0.354	—	0.415	0.866
	Weather	—	—	—	—	0.736	0.415	—	0.593
	Device	—	—	—	—	—	0.866	0.593	—

2.2.1   THE RELATIONSHIP BETWEEN CONTEXT DIMENSIONS

Personal Attributes and Physical Environment

The participants' personal attributes and their physical environment do not correlate with each other, except in regard to gender and search place. We made further analysis of these two dimensions (Tables 2.12 and 2.13).

Table 2.12: Gender and search place

	At home or dorm (p-value)	In workplace (p=-value)	In study place (p-value)	In public (p-value)	On the way (p-value)	On vacation (p-value)
Gender	0.967	0.912	0.000**	0.006**	0.008**	0.017*
Note: * < 0.05, ** p < 0.01.						

Table 2.13: Relationships between gender and search place

	In study place (%)	In public (%)	On the way (%)	On vacation (%)
Male	43.7	3.0	4.4	0
Female	22.2	10.8	12.7	4.1

Tables 2.12 and 2.13 show that four kinds of places were closely connected with gender. Specifically, male participants tend to conduct mobile searches in study areas, whereas female participants tend to perform mobile searches when they are traveling, in public, and on vacation. Mobile search is more popular in female participants' daily lives, while male participants prefer to use mobile devices when studying.

Personal Attributes and Social Environment

The detailed correlation results are listed in Table 2.14. "P" stands for partially correlated, i.e., a subdivision of a certain dimension correlates with another dimension or a subdivision of the dimension.

Table 2.14: Personal attributes and social environment

Context		Personal Attributes (p-value)			
		Gender	Age	Grade	Major
Personal attributes	Gender	—	—	—	—
	Age	—	—	—	—
	Grade	—	—	—	—
	Major	—	—	—	—
Social environments	Activity	0.000**	0.357	0.399	0.610
	Relations	0.138	0.231	0.786	0.577
	Importance	0.116	0.573	0.396	0.150
	Portal	P	0.717	0.202	0.598
Context		Social environment (p-value)			
		Activity	Relations	Importance	Portal
Personal attributes	Gender	0.000**	0.138	0.116	P
	Age	0.357	0.231	0.573	0.717
	Grade	0.399	0.786	0.396	0.202
	Major	0.610	0.577	0.150	0.598
Social environments	Activity	—	0.000**	0.000**	—
	Relations	0.000**	—	0.633	0.171
	Importance	0.000**	0.633	—	0.573
	Portal	—	0.171	0.573	—
Note: * < 0.05, ** $p < 0.01$.					

(i) Gender and activity

Among the personal attributes of the participants, gender and current activity have significant correlations with one another, meaning that men are more likely to do mobile searches when studying, whereas women often carry out mobile searches when they are on a break. This reveals some of the different functions of mobile search based on gender (Table 2.15).

Table 2.15: Relationships between gender and activity			
		Activity		
		Top 1 (%)	Top 2 (%)	Top 3 (%)
Gender	Male	On break (55.6)	Studying (37.0)	Others (4.4)
	Female	On break (61.9)	Studying (18.4)	Others (7.9)

(ii) Gender and search portal

We found that gender and search portal are partly correlated (Table 2.16). Transportation, social, and shopping APPs significantly correlate with gender. Male participants are more likely to conduct mobile searches via social and shopping APPs. This phenomenon might have something to do with the different information concerns between male and female participants, causing them to choose corresponding search portals.

Table 2.16: Gender and search portal	
Search portal	Gender (p-value)
Browser	0.001**
Video APP	0.239
Music APP	0.627
Transportation APP	0.036*
Social APP	0.000**
Shopping APP	0.021*
Application store	0.624
Reference APP	0.798
Note: * < 0.05, ** p < 0.01.	

(iii) Activity and relations

Current activity and relations significantly correlate with each other, as shown in Table 2.17. Participants were often alone when they were on a break, studying, or working, whereas shopping, traveling, and doing other activities occurred with friends.

Table 2.17: Relationship between activity and relations		
Alone (%)	With friends (%)	
On break	49.3	—
Working	55.0	—
Studying	50.0	—
Shopping	—	42.9
Traveling	—	85.7
Others	—	38.7

(iv) Activity and importance

Current activity and importance of a search task significantly correlate with one another, as shown in Table 2.18. The search tasks performed while participants were on a break or doing casual activities were usually unimportant or non-urgent, while the tasks were more important when they were working, studying, and traveling.

Table 2.18: Relationships between activity and task importance

	Important (%)	Neutral (%)	Unimportant (%)
On break	15.9	45.9	38.1
Working	45.0	45.0	10.0
Studying	40.7	48.1	11.1
Shopping	28.6	71.4	0
Traveling	50.0	28.6	21.4
Others	29.0	32.3	38.7

Physical Environment and Social Environment

The detailed correlation results are listed in Table 2.19. The "A" in the table stands for all correlated, which means all subdivisions of a certain dimension correlate with another dimension or a subdivision of the dimension.

Table 2.19: Physical environment and social environment

Context		Physical Environments (p-value)			
		Time	Place	Weather	Device
Physical environments	Time	—	—	0.736	—
	Place	—	—	0.415	0.866
	Weather	0.736	0.415	—	0.593
	Device	—	0.866	0.593	—
Social environments	Activity	0.593	0.000**	0.559	0.137
	Relations	0.586	A	0.374	0.347
	Importance	0.206	—	0.412	0.631
	Portal	—	—	—	0.186

Table 2.19 continued

Context		Social environment (p-value)			
		Activity	Relations	Importance	Portal
Physical environments	Time	0.593	0.586	0.206	—
	Place	0.000**	A	—	—
	Weather	0.559	0.374	0.412	—
	Device	0.137	0.037	0.061	0.186
Social environments	Activity	—	0.000**	0.000**	—
	Relations	0.000**	—	0.633	0.171
	Importance	0.000**	0.633	—	0.573
	Portal	—	0.171	0.573	—
Note: * < 0.05, ** p < 0.01.					

(i) Place and activity

As shown in Table 2.19, search place and current activity all correlate with one another. Further analysis is shown in Table 2.20. The activities the participants were engaged in depended greatly on the function of the place. For example, they were often taking a break when at a friend's home or dormitory, whereas they were studying when in a place of study.

Table 2.20: Relationships between place and activity

		Activity		
		Top 1 (%)	Top 2 (%)	Top 3 (%)
Place	At home or dorm	On break (80.5)	Studying (13.4)	Working (3.7)
	Female	On break (61.9)	Studying (18.4)	Others (7.9)
	In workplace	Working (50.0)	On break (31.3)	Studying (12.5)
	In study place	Studying (58.9)	On break (34.1)	Others (4.7)
	In public	On break (44.7)	Others (28.9)	Shopping (10.5)
	On the way	On break (50.0)	Traveling (23.9)	Others (23.9)
	On vacation	Traveling (84.6)	On break (15.4)	—

Search place and relations of the participant are significantly correlated. To be as specific as possible, we performed a cross tabulation analysis between every place and its relations (Tables 2.21 and 2.22).

Table 2.21: Place and relations

Place	Relations (p-value)
At home or dorm	0.001**
In workplace	0.000**
In study place	0.000**
In public	0.037*
On the way	0.001**
On vacation	0.000**

Note: * < 0.05, ** p < 0.01.

Table 2.22: Relationships between place and relations

	Top 1 (%)	Top 2 (%)	Top 3 (%
At home or dorm	Alone (50.4)	With classmates (23.2)	With friends (19.5)
In workplace	Alone (43.8)	With friends (31.3)	With workmates (12.5)
In study place	Alone (47.3)	With classmates (38.0)	With friends (10.9)
In public	With friends (42.1)	Alone (26.3)	With classmates (23.7)
On the way	Alone (60.9)	With friends (32.6)	With strangers (7.7)
On vacation	With friends (92.3)	Alone (7.7)	—

As shown in Table 2.21, there are significant correlations between search places and current relations when conducting a mobile search; Table 2.22 shows the correlations more specifically. Participants were alone when at home or in a dormitory, in their workplace, and in a place of study. They were often with their friends when in public or on vacation. This is related to the characteristics and functions of the different places.

2.2.2 IMPACT OF CONTEXT ON MOBILE SEARCH INFORMATION NEEDS

Information need and mobile search context are both parts of information search behaviors. Information need is expected to be related to the various attributes of the participants and their surroundings. The correlation analysis results are shown in Table 2.23. The "A" in the table stands for all correlated, which means all subdivisions of a certain dimension correlated with another dimension or a subdivision of the dimension. If the users tended to search for certain information via various portals at the same time, we made analyses of the information need and every portal.

Table 2.23: Information need and mobile search context

Category	Mobile Search Context Dimensions	Correlations (p-value)
Personal attributes of the participant	Gender	0.000**
	Age	0.325
	Grade	0.139
	Major	0.314
Physical environment of the participant	Time	0.232
	Place	——
	Weather	0.412
	Device	0.253
Social environment of the participant	Activity	0.002**
	Relations	0.577
	Importance	0.032*
	Portal	A

Note: * < 0.05, ** p < 0.01.

The participants' social environment has significant correlations with their information needs, while their physical environment does not. To get a better understanding of these correlations, we made the following additional analyses.

Information Need Type and Personal Attributes

Table 2.24 shows that the information need type has significant correlations with gender, which means that male and female participants have different information need types. In addition, age, grade, and major do not have any correlation with information need types.

Table 2.24: Top three relationships between information need and gender

Gender	Top 1 (%)	Top 2 (%)	Top 3 (%)
Male	Arts (23.0)	Social sciences (14.1)	Natural sciences (14.1)
Female	Arts (24.8)	Social sciences (18.7)	Recreation (10.2)

The results in Table 2.24 show that both male and female participants are mainly interested in arts information. In addition, female participants care more about social sciences and recreation information, whereas male participants prefer natural science information. This phenomenon shows that information needs differ between male and female participants, and that female participants tend to do mobile searching when relaxed.

Information Need Type and Social Environment

Social environment includes current activity, relations, task importance, and portal. Table 2.23 indicates that all of the dimensions except relations had significant correlations with information need types. To better understand these correlations, we provide cross tabulation in Tables 2.25–2.28.

Table 2.25: Top three relationships between information need and activity			
Activity	**Top 1 (%)**	**Top 2 (%)**	**Top 3 (%)**
On break	Arts (24.4)	Science (Social Sciences) (18.1)	Recreation (8.1)
Working	Arts (40.0)	Science (Social Sciences) (30.0)	Reference (15.0)
Studying	Arts (23.1)	Science (Natural Sciences) (15.7)	Science (Social Science) (13.9)
Shopping	Recreation (57.1)	News (14.3)	Science (Social Science) (14.3)
Traveling	Recreation (28.6)	Arts (21.4)	Science (Social Science) (14.3)
Others	Arts (22.6)	Science (Social Sciences) (16.1)	Science (Natural Sciences) (12.9)

The activity and information need types significantly correlated with one another (Table 2.25). Participants cared about recreation information when taking a break, reference information when working, and natural science information when studying. In addition, participants preferred arts information when traveling.

The search task may occasionally be important or urgent. As shown in Table 2.23, search task importance significantly correlates with information need types. When searching for social science, economics and celebrities are considered important by participants, while culture and art are considered unimportant.

Table 2.26: Top three relationships between information need and importance			
Task Importance	**Top 1 (%)**	**Top 2 (%)**	**Top 3 (%)**
Important	Science (Social Sciences) (24.7)	Arts (16.7)	Recreation (11.4)
Neutral	Arts (27.5)	Science (Social Sciences) (10.8)	Science (Natural Science) (10.3)
Unimportant	Science (Social Sciences) (28.0)	Arts (25.8)	Region (8.0)

Search portal and information need types are correlated, but the prominent correlation between each search portal and information need types is slightly different, as shown in Tables 2.27 and 2.28.

Table 2.27: Information need and search portal	
Search Portal	**Correlations (p-value)**
Browser	0.000**
Video APP	0.007**
Music APP	0.000**
Transportation APP	0.000**
Social APP	0.000**
Shopping APP	0.000**
Application store	0.000**
Reference APP	0.023*
Note: * < 0.05, ** p < 0.01.	

Table 2.28: Top three relationships between search portal and information need types

Search portal	Top 1 (%)	Top 2 (%)	Top 3 (%)
Browser	Arts (23.6)	Science (Social Sciences) (18.4)	Science (Natural Science) (9.2)
Video APP	Arts (63.2)	Recreation (10.5)	Science (Social Science) (5.3)
Music APP	Arts (100)	——	——
Transportation APP	Transportation (47.6)	Recreation (33.3)	Others (14.3)
Social APP	Science (Social Sciences) (45.9)	Social (16.2)	Arts (13.5)
Shopping APP	Shopping (57.1)	Recreation (35.7)	Social (3.6)
Application store	Computers (80.0)	Recreation (20.0)	——
Reference APP	Arts (66.7)	Science (Natural Science) (25.0)	Others (8.3)

As the above tables show, mobile search portal and information need have significant correlations. Besides arts and social science, the information searched through browsers is also about natural science, so browsers could serve as a good search portal for participants' daily studying. The information searched through video APPs and music APPs is mostly about arts and recreation, and this conforms to the resource characteristics of the search portal itself. When setting traveling and traffic, social networking, shopping, and learning APP as portals, the information need types are consistent with the characteristics of those search portals. When participants use APP stores, they generally search computer and recreation APPs.

2.2.3   IMPACT OF CONTEXT ON MOBILE SEARCH QUERIES

We obtained query frequency data from the structured diaries and the search logs, and counted the query frequency at different periods. Table 2.29 shows the correlation analysis results, in which only time and place are significantly correlated with query frequency.

We divided one 24-hour day into 4 periods—00:00–06:00, 06:00–12:00, 12:00–18:00, and 18:00–24:00. We chose this time division to equate the length of the four periods and make 00:00 the beginning of a day. As mobile searching is convenient, instant, and the users may conduct it at any time, we did not take mealtime into consideration. However, the time division we used might not be optimal as it cut through mealtimes, which may have influenced the analysis.

Category	Mobile Search Context Dimensions	Correlations (p-value)
Personal attributes of the participant	Gender	0.351
	Age	0.271
	Grade	0.577
	Major	0.326
Physical environment of the participant	Time	0.000**
	Place	0.000**
	Weather	0.699
	Device	0.154
Social environment of the participant	Activity	0.190
	Relations	0.280
	Importance	0.214
	Portal	0.881

Table 2.29: Search query and context

Note: * < 0.05, ** p < 0.01.

The places here contain six specific locations: home or dormitory, workplace, place of study, in public, in transit, and on vacation. In order to understand query frequency in four periods and six locations, we provide two cross tabulations, as shown in Tables 2.30 and 2.31.

Table 2.30: Top two relationships between time and query frequency

Time	Query frequency (%)
18:00–24:00	44.2
12:00–18:00	40.0

Table 2.31: Top two relationships between place and query frequency

Place	Query frequency (%)
Home or dormitory	54.7
Study place	28.7

Note: Percentage in Tables 2.30 and 2.31 both referred to the ratio of query frequency to all queries.

Table 2.30 indicates that about 44.2% of the queries appear between 18:00 and 24:00, and 40% between 12:00 and 18:00. Furthermore, the place and query frequency have significant correlations. About 54.7% of the queries were formulated at home or in the dormitory, and 28.7% in a place of study. This might have something to do with the college students' lifestyle—they often stay up late and are active in the afternoon, while dormitories and places of study are two main locations of their college life.

2.2.4   IMPACT OF CONTEXT ON MOBILE SEARCH EFFECTIVENESS

In Experiment I, we did not evaluate the users' mobile search performance. The users' emotions can affect their search effectiveness. Emotion changes in a mobile search means the change of a user's emotion after searching for information on a mobile device. It is divided into three categories: better, worse, and no change.

As shown in Table 2.32, among the 12 dimensions, only gender, task importance, and portal significantly correlate with emotion change. It also shows that social environment more closely correlates with emotion changes than the other two context categories. We examined every search portal with respect to emotion change and learned that all the search portals correlate with emotion change to some degree. The "P" in the table stands for partially correlated, i.e., a subdivision of a certain dimension correlates with another dimension or a subdivision of the dimension.

Table 2.32: Emotion change and context		
Category	Mobile Search Context Dimensions	Correlations (p-value)
Personal attributes of the participant	Gender	0.013*
	Age	0.342
	Grade	0.451
	Major	0.182
Physical environment of the participant	Time	0.147
	Place	——
	Weather	0.723
	Device	0.247
Social environment of the participant	Activity	0.108
	Relations	0.230
	Importance	0.000**
	Portal	P

Emotion Change and Personal Attributes

Among the four dimensions of personal attributes, only gender has significant correlations with emotion change; we made further analysis of the relationships between them.

Table 2.33 shows that men's emotion changes are more significant than those of women. This might be due to the information for which they searched. For example, the women tended to search for recreation information, while the men preferred natural science. Men became happier when they obtained knowledge, while the women focused more on fun.

Table 2.33: Relationships between gender and emotion change

Gender	Better (%)	Neither (%)	Worse (%)
Male	42.2	47.4	10.4
Female	28.9	61.9	9.2

Emotion Change and Social Environment

As Table 2.34 shows, emotion changes of the participants and task importance are significantly correlated with one another. Emotion change becomes more obvious as the search task becomes more important or urgent. We conclude that emotion changes vary depending on whether the important information need is satisfied.

Table 2.34: Relationship between emotion change and task importance

Task importance	Better (%)	Neither (%)	Worse (%)
Important	45.6	36.8	17.5
Neutral	33.8	58.3	7.8
Unimportant	20.5	74.2	5.3

We analyzed the correlation between every search portal and emotion change, finding that some search portals are significantly correlated with emotion change. As seen in Tables 2.35 and 2.36, 89% of the participants' moods did not become worse when searching through a browser. This illustrates the utility of the browser for the participants. When using a social APP, the participants also did not have dramatic changes in emotion.

Table 2.35: Emotion change and search portal

Search Portal	Correlations (p-value)
Browser	0.032*
Video APP	0.198
Music APP	0.321
Transportation APP	0.740
Social APP	0.021*
Shopping APP	0.586
Application store	0.390
Reference APP	0.052
Note: * < 0.05, ** $p < 0.01$.	

Table 2.36: Relationships between emotion change and search portal			
Search portal	**Better (%)**	**Neither (%)**	**Worse (%)**
Browser	35.0	54.0	11.0
Social software	13.5	78.4	8.1

2.2.5   MULTI-DIMENSIONAL MODEL OF MOBILE SEARCH BEHAVIORS

Based on the analysis of the impact of mobile search motivations and context on search behaviors, we built a multi-dimensional model of mobile search behaviors and their influencing factors (Figure 2.9). After cross analysis and regression analysis, we did not detect specific causality. As the data did not conform to the regression analysis model, we cannot carry out regression analysis. Therefore, the line in the Figure 2.9 had no directivity and degree of influence, indicating relevance only.

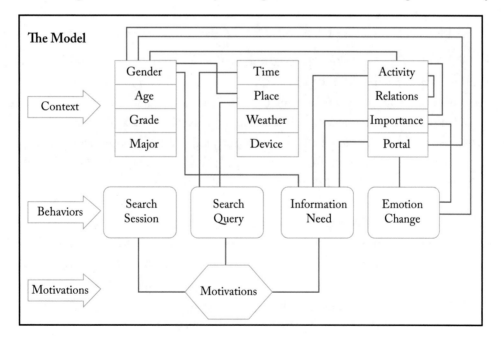

Figure 2.9: The motivation- and context-based mobile search behavior model.

Search motivations affect mobile search behaviors in terms of mobile search sessions, mobile search queries, and information needs. In contextual dimensions, the time and place of a mobile search correlate with the mobile search query. In addition, gender, search activity, search task importance, and portal all have significant correlations with information need types. Correlations among the contextual dimensions are also significant. Gender, time, place, search activity, relations, task importance, and portal correlate with each other in several ways, and the other dimensions have no significant correlations. In short, mobile search is a successive process involving mobile search motivation, context, and mobile search behaviors.

2.3   DESIGNING CONTEXT-BASED MOBILE SEARCH TASK COLLECTION

The prevalence of mobile search has triggered more studies on mobile search tasks, such as how they can affect mobile search behavior (Baron et al., 2016). However, there is a lack of focus in these studies on mobile search task design. Current evaluation frameworks also seldom have tracks specifically for mobile search. Previous studies have found that there are many differences between mobile and desktop searching; therefore, tasks designed for desktop search should not be directly used for mobile search, and it is important to design mobile-specific search tasks. In this section, we design the mobile search task collection considering context factors, as discussed in Section 2.2.

2.3.1   EXTRACTING AND EXPANDING MOBILE SEARCH TOPICS

Inspired by the TREC test collection construction method and introducing contextual factors, we designed the mobile search tasks in two parts. The procedure is shown in Figure 2.10.

The core task design derives from a small group of users' real mobile searches in Experiment I. We recorded the most memorable mobile search of each user in a day as the core task collection. The characteristics of mobile search behaviors were analyzed and the context factors affecting mobile search behaviors were extracted from Experiment I. However, the number of users' real search tasks is limited in Experiment I and there are many combinations of context factors. Therefore, expanded task designs were identified from a large group of users' surveys based on context extracted in Section 2.2. We filtered contextual factors according to the users' selection of each contextual factor in the survey. Finally, we decided upon the most effective contextual factors and combined them in different ways to stimulate users' mobile search tasks and context. The core tasks and the expanded tasks were edited under the same structure. Since the purpose of our work is to design mobile web search tasks rather than to evaluate information retrieval systems, only mobile search topics and the ground-truth are designed without the document set.

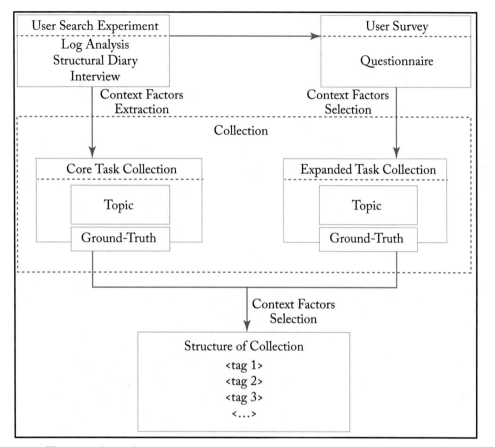

Figure 2.10: The procedure of mobile search task design.

2.3.2 SELECTING CONTEXT DIMENSIONS OF MOBILE SEARCH TASK

Core Task Design Based on Real Situation

In Experiment I, a total of 450 real search tasks with contextual information were collected as the raw data of the core tasks. Three context categories of information need, physical environment, and social environment, and 12 contextual factors of mobile searching were extracted from Table 2.10.

The subjects of the search tasks were classified according to the categories of Wikipedia contents; for example, searches about anodyne medicine can be classified in the health category. These tasks were divided into 16 primary classes and 83 subclasses. The mobile search task types are based on search intentions proposed by Rose and Levinson (2004), which were classified with the consideration of queries of participants' search logs, the information need description, and answers provided by participants. The task types were classified into three primary classes: Navigation Task,

Information Task, and Resource Task. Each class of the task type was divided into subclasses. The definition and examples of each task type are shown in Table 2.37.

Table 2.37: The task type				
Task type		**Description**	**Example**	**Number of tasks**
Navigation		The goal of the task is to get the specific known website.	iQIYI website	17
Information	List	The goal of the task is to get a list of plausible suggested websites or the search result lists, each of which might be helpful to achieve some unspecified goal.	Trains of the Changsha railway station	45
	Advice	The goal of the task is to get advice, ideas, suggestions, or instructions.	Methods of cultivating small plants form litchi	57
	Location	The goal of the task is to find out where some service or product can be obtained.	Location of "Wal-Mart"	6
	Undirected	The goal of the task is to learn anything/everything about the topic.	Information about Rhode Island	136
	Directed — Closed	The goal of the task is to get an answer to a question that has a single, unambiguous answer.	Price of the perfume on Amazon	40
	Directed — Open	The goal of the task is to get an open-ended question, or one with unconstrained depth.	Reasons of paralysis of a website	38
Resource	Interact	The goal of the task is to interact with a resource using another program/service available. on the mobile phone	Search for the weather by voice search	19
	Entertainment	The goal of the task is to be entertained by viewing items available on the result page.	Batman and Spider-man	44
	Obtain	The goal of the task is to obtain a resource that can be looked at on the Web but cannot be downloaded.	Search for the dark photos	40
	Download	The goal of the task is to download a useful resource on the mobile phone.	Download the application "Gmail"	6

Finally, the core tasks consist of 450 tasks with 35 failed and repeated tasks. The ground-truth was provided by participants with their satisfied search results. The results include URLs and specific content.

Expanded Task Design based on Simulated Situation

Outline of Questionnaire about Search Tasks

(1) Information Need

1. What topic of information do you want to search for? (*5-level Likert scales*)

2. What category of your mobile search tasks do you conduct? (*5-level Likert scales*)

3. What is your search motivation using mobile phones? (*5-level Likert scales*)

4. What is your emotion in the current situation? (*5-level Likert scales*)

(2) Physical Environment

1. How often do you search on mobile searches in the following locations? (*5-level Likert scales*)

(3) Social Environment

1. How often do you search on mobile searches in the following activities? (*5-level Likert scales*)

2. What kind of APPs do you use in your mobile search process? (*5-level Likert scales*)

- -

Physical Enfironment:

How often do you search on mobile searches in the following locations?
   (1→5: wish of searching from weak to strong)

	1	2	3	4	5
At home or a dormitory					
In a study place					
On the way					
In public					
In the work place					
On vacation					
Others					

Figure 2.11: Outline and a segment of the questionnaire.

Since core tasks were designed based on a small number of users, we aimed to expand the number of tasks collected. It was difficult to obtain all the contextual factors for a large-scale real mobile search; thus, the questionnaire was used as the basic method of a simulated situation to design expanded tasks. What's more, not all of the 12 context factors identified in the core tasks had an impact on mobile search. According to the analysis of the context influence on query frequency through statistical analysis by crosstabs and one-way ANOVA, search time, search device, current relations, information material, and current weather have no relation to mobile information seeking behavior. The seven context factors that affect mobile search behaviors are search place, current activity, search motivation, task importance, search application, topic subject, and task type (Wu et al., 2016b; 2016c). Among them, the topic subject was refined into the subtopic, and 20 subtopics with over 10 tasks in the core tasks were selected. All the selected context factors were used to design the questionnaire. In the questionnaire, a 5-level Likert scale (scores of 1–5 ranging from the weakest to the strongest) was utilized for users to evaluate the importance of these context factors in their mobile search. The outline and a segment of the questionnaire is shown in Figure 2.11. The questionnaire was distributed online and the respondents were all university students. A total of 500 valid respondents were available among the 530 participants.

Expanded tasks were designed by using the questionnaire results completed collaboratively by three experts majoring in Library and Information Science. For the seven context factors, the average score of each was calculated and ranked from high to low. The context factors of topic subject and task type were decided first, since these two factors had the most memorable effect on mobile search behavior. A total of 550 expanded tasks were designed. All three experts confirmed web search results to establish the ground-truth in order to guarantee it was closely related to the task. When disagreement occurred, the three experts had a discussion and came to an agreement.

2.3.3   RELEVANCE JUDGMENT AND GROUND TRUTH

The Results of Core Tasks

The core tasks consist of 450 topics and the number of topics was calculated by context factors of subject, task type, search place, current activity, and search application, respectively.

Since the subject of the core tasks was composed of too many subclasses, we only described the number of topics using 16 primary classes. Results show that the distribution of search topics is scattered and the most-searched-for categories fall under the subjects of art, computers, and social science. However, some subjects like social science are composed of 50 topics of subclass celebrity, which is more than half, indicating that the subjects of mobile search tasks are relatively concentrated.

For the task type, as shown in Table 2.37, information task is the primary type of mobile search task, accounting for 71.56%, followed by resource task with 24.22%. Navigation task only accounts for 3.78%. In all types of information task, undirected (30.2%) is the most common, indicating that the information need of mobile search users was usually unclear. Meanwhile, the transition of the task type existed with only two cases. One was from "information task/list" to "resource task/entertainment" when the user searched for the film "My God." Another was from "information task/undirected" to "information task/list" when the user searched for the song "People Strong without Fat Horses," indicating that through the process of the search, the target became clearer.

For the rest of the three context factors—current activity, search place, and search application—Table 2.38 lists the number of topics that are greater than or equal to 10. Mobile search at a family's/relative's/friend's home/dormitory had the highest frequency. The second highest was at a place of study. Searching during times of rest and study is consistent with the lifestyles of university students. The search entrance focused on the browser. Some topics contain more than two search places and search applications due to a transition that occurred.

Table 2.38: Current activity, search place, and search application of the topics in core tasks

Current Activity	Number of Topics	Search place	Number of Topics	Search Application	Number of Topics
On break	270	At home or dormitory	230	Browser	312
Studying	108	In study place	108	Social software	31
Others	31	On the way	33	Shopping software	18
Working	20	In public	30	Transportation software	17
Traveling	14	At home or dormitory/ In study place	12	Video software	15
		In workplace	10	Music software	14
				Group buy software	10

The Results of Core Expanded Tasks

A total of 500 valid responses to the questionnaire were received, with 46% of the respondents male and 54% female. The distribution of education level was concentrated, with 73% undergraduate students, 25.8% graduate students, and 1.2% Ph.D. students; 68.4% were between 20 and 30 years old. The range of majors was wide, including those majoring in law, business administration, chemistry, accounting, finance, economics, information science, microelectronics science, physics, insurance, engineering, etc. Users having high and relatively high frequency of mobile searching accounted for 77%, indicating that users regularly search for information with mobile phones in their daily life.

Figure 2.12 shows users' mobile search subjects. News and Music were the most frequent search intentions, whereas Economy and Business were the least common search intentions. The number of topics in the expanded tasks was allocated based on the average value of users' search intention. There are five levels. When the average value is less than or equal to 2.5 (such as Economy and Business), the number of topics is 10. When the average value is more than 2.5 and less than or equal to 3 (such as Disease and Symptom, Science, Smartphone), the number of topics is 20. When the average value is more than 3 and less than or equal to 3.5 (such as Examination, Literature, Language), the number of topic numbers is 30; when the average value is more than 3.5 (such as Music and News), the number of topics is 40. There are a total of 550 topics in the expanded tasks.

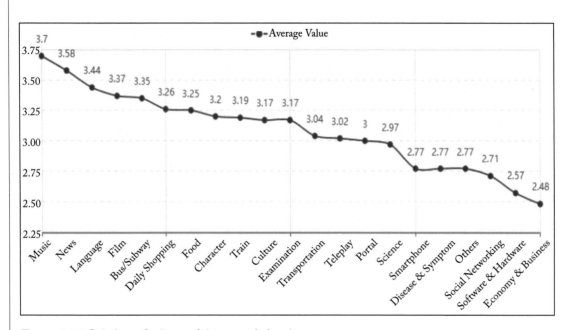

Figure 2.12: Subclass of subject of the expanded tasks.

Figure 2.13 shows other context factors of the expanded tasks. Except for Resource/Interact, the average values of all the other task types are over 3. The average values of the main task types—Resource/Download, Resource/Obtain, and Navigation—are over 3.5. The average values of Information/Directed, Information/Advice, and Information/Location are higher than that of Information/Undirected and Information/List, indicating university users require more specific information. The search places are mainly at a home/dormitory, at a place of study, and while traveling, and the search behaviors were mainly conducted in the process of resting, studying, and traveling. The main entry point of mobile search is the browser APPs, which is consistent to the core tasks, and the second is the SNS APPs. Study APPs ranked third, indicating a need for study-related information is significant for college students.

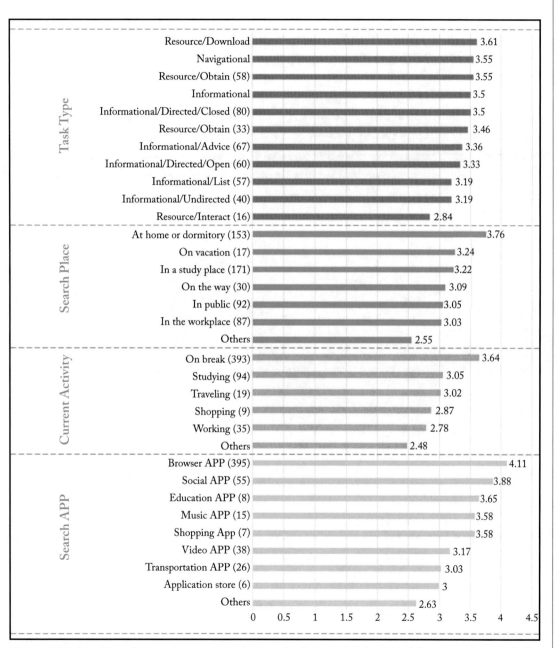

Figure 2.13: Search application, current activity, search place, and task type of the topics in expanded tasks.

2.3.4 STRUCTURE OF MOBILE SEARCH TASK COLLECTION

The core task and expanded task share the same structure written in XML (see Figure 2.14). Referring to the TREC Topic structure, four tags—<number>, <title>, <description>, and <narrative>—were selected as part of the mobile search task structure. "C" means the topic is from core tasks, and "E" means the topic is from expended tasks. Among the seven context factors, search motivation and task importance are related to personnel, so these two are excluded from the task structure. Finally, only five tags—<search place>, <current activity>, <search application>, <subject>, and <task type>—were used to describe the context in the task structure. Among them, the subject was classified into <primary class> as the first class and <subclass> as the second class. Task type was classified into three classes—<primary type>, <subtype>, and <third type>—if the task type had three levels.

```
<topic lang="ch"<
<subject>
  <primary class>Recreation</primary class>
  <subclass>food and restaurant</subclass>
</subject>
<number>E131</number>
<title>Shijiuguan Restaurant</title>
<description>search the address of Shijiuguan Restaurant</description>
<narrative>search the specific address information including the street name and the
building number</narrative>
<task type>
  <primary type>Information</primary type>
  <subtype>Location</subtype>
</task type>
<search place>on public</search place>
<current activity>waiting for someone</current activity>
<search application>shopping APP</search application>
</topic>
<answer>
  <number>E131</number>
  <URL>http://www.dianping.com/shop/17185534</URL>
  <source>Dianping APP</source>
  <content>No. 55,Changchun Street, Hankou (next to the relic of the Eight Route Army
  Office, across from Wuhan Tiandi Shopping Center, near the Huangpulu Station, No.1
  subway line)</content>
</answer>
```

Figure 2.14: An example of the task structure in XML.

In terms of the structure of the ground-truth, the tag <number> is consistent with the tag <number> in the task structure. Also, since the results are from a web search, the URLs of the results were recorded in the tag <URL>, the name of the website was recorded in the tag <source>, and the most related content of the topic was described in the tag <content>.

2.3.5   COMPARISON OF CONTEXT-BASED MOBILE SEARCH TASKS WITH OTHERS

This section introduces the context for designing 1,000 mobile search tasks. Comparing TREC topics and One Click topics, ours describes different aspects of the search topics. Context factors like task type in mobile tasks can make information needs clearer, especially for mobile search. As the example shows in Figure 2.15, when the search entrance is limited to traveling and traffic applications, the application will provide users with traffic- and map-related information. The search entrance is not limited in One Click and the general search engine is used; therefore, in addition to traffic and map information, it is possible for users to view myriad text information, such as the profile and development of Kobe Central Library, etc. When the current activity is limited to traveling, the system will recommend more suitable traffic routes to the users, while One Click is unable to do that.

TREC	`<topic number = "1" type = "faceted">`
	`<query> feta cheese preservatives </query>`
	`<description>`
	`   Find information on which substances are used to extend the shelf life of feta`
	`cheese`
	`<description>`
	`<subtopic number = "1" type = "inf">`
	`   Find information on which substances are used to extend the shelf life of feta`
	`cheese`
	`<subtopic>`
	`</topic>`

Mobile Search Tasks	`<topic lang = "ch">`
	`<subject>`
	`<primary class> transportation </primary class>`
	`<subclass> bus or subway </subclass>`
	`<number> 104 </number>`
	`<title> stop </title>`
	`<description>search for the bus stops within 100 meters in Pudong New District,`
	`Shanghai Jia Bang Road </description>`
	`<narrative> include the name of bus stops and stopping bus lines </narrative>`
	`<task type>`
	`<search place> on the way </search place>`
	`<current activity> on break </current activity>`
	`<search application> Transportation application </search application>`
	`</topic>`

One Click	`<query ID = "6">`
	`<query type> celebrity </query type)`
	`<search intent number = "1"`
	`<query string> central library of Kobe City </query string>`

Figure 2.15: The comparison of three tasks.

Without context factors, the search results would be more diverse and harder for the user to decide on. If the search place changed from "in public" to "on the way," the information need may change from simply wanting the address of the restaurant to also wanting the bus transfer or driving route information. Also, if the current activity changes from "waiting for someone" to "resting," the information need might change from wanting the exact address leading someone to a specific restaurant to just taking a look at the address to see where it is. The same thing would happen when changing search applications. The shopping APP would give address information as well as the telephone, picture, and evaluation information of the restaurant, while other applications such as search engine would only give the general address information. Therefore, different contexts would change to different search tasks and provide more targeted information, even though they were of the same topic subject.

2.4   SUMMARY

In this chapter, we primarily studied users' mobile search strategies in natural settings, built the multi-dimensional context model of mobile search, and designed the mobile search task.

Regarding the increasing popularity of mobile search, it is notable that users utilize multiple languages to form queries in a mobile search. English queries and Chinese-English mixed queries account for high proportions, which not only reflects that users have been accustomed to searching in multiple languages, but also indicates that search engines are providing increasingly accurate support for multilingual queries. Previous studies on mobile search behavior note that information user search had a wide range of topics. In this experiment, we arrived at a similar conclusion. It can also be found that college students focus on several particular topics. For example, they concentrate more on searching for "reference" and "science" than ordinary users. Additionally, the numbers of queries submitted by participants and the search sessions in this experiment are larger than what previous studies reported, which indicates that users with higher information literacy have higher frequencies of mobile searching. Comparing our study with previous research, we notice that users more commonly used a single query to search in this experiment. At the same time, the frequency of long search sessions is also higher in this experiment, suggesting that mobile search has become a convenient and fast choice for users to search for web information, and also indicating that users have begun to perform more complex search tasks with mobile devices. Furthermore, by investigating features of query language, query reformulation, search session length, cross-application distribution of search sessions, and so on, it can be found that participants have more diverse search strategies, which reflects that participants with higher information literacy have better search abilities.

Based on the analysis of mobile search behavior, we understand how search motivations and context influence mobile search behaviors. Our results show that about three-fourths of mobile search sessions are driven by a single motivation, while a quarter are driven by multiple motivations. Different search motivations have the tendency to cross and converge, especially among searches driven by curiosity, time killing, and learning. Queries in search sessions influenced by three motivations tend to be repeated less frequently than queries in life service, which suggests that the former three stimulate more types of information needs, while life service motivation is more stable and uniform. Information needs are found to be mainly driven by three types of motivation: curiosity, learning, and life service. No significant correlations are found between emotion changes and motivations. In addition, we also find that information search behaviors significantly correlate with the multidimensional context and motivation. Gender, search activity, task importance, and portal all have significant correlations with information need type, and information needs driven by different motivations are diverse. Furthermore, the correlations among the dimensional context are significant. Gender, time, place, search activity, relations, search task importance, and portal dimensions are all correlated in several ways, and the other dimensions have no significant correlation.

Through the mobile search experiment and survey, this chapter analyzed the characteristics of users' mobile search topics and determined the context factors of mobile search, including the subject, task type, search place, current activity, and search entrance as the main factors influencing the mobile task design. Inspired by the TREC design, we developed a total of 1,000 mobile search tasks consisting of 450 core tasks from real situations and 550 expanded tasks from simulated situations. The design of context-based mobile search tasks offers a new way of thinking about task design. The mobile search tasks in this chapter include users' information need tendencies and context factors; thus, combining mobile tasks with contexts can provide users with personalized advice and information recommendation. Additionally, mobile search tasks in this paper are varied. The data of this chapter includes not only logs of a single system, but also logs of APP usage, which can help to contrast search behavior on different applications. The mobile search tasks of our research are openly available for all researchers to support related studies.

CHAPTER 3

Mobile Search Behaviors and APP Usage

These days, users can utilize many different APPs to get information on their mobile phones. Since APPs have become the main interaction method for users when they are on their personal smart devices, it is necessary to study users' mobile search behaviors on various APPs. In this chapter, we study the relationship between mobile search and APP usage. This topic was addressed by Experiment I, introduced in Section 1.4.

In Experiment I, we collected users' mobile phone usage, including two datasets: Application and Mobile Search. We exported the data by creating an association between the Application dataset and the Keyboard dataset using the timestamp.

3.1 APP TOPICS AND MOBILE SEARCH

A search session is a process in which a user submits a single query or multiple queries through a search engine to satisfy their information needs over a period of time (Wu and Liang, 2015). Unlike traditional desktop search, the current mobile search is done mainly through different APPs. The mobile search session contains users' mobile records (over a period of time), such as query text records (Daoud et al., 2009), APP usage records (Carrascal and Church 2015), and other mobile touch interactions records (Han et al., 2015a), which are important for analyzing mobile search behavior. In the mobile search session, studies that combine users' multiple APP interactions with mobile search can assist understanding of the relationship between mobile search and APP usage. Cross-analysis of users' search topic, search time, and the APP topics also allows for understanding users' search strategies when using different APPs, as well as their search preferences. In this section, we study the relationship between the APP interaction and the mobile search session, and the relationship between the time factor, search topics, and APP topics.

3.1.1 IDENTIFYING APP TOPICS AND APP CHAIN

Through the data collection from Experiment I, a total of 1,023,709 data records were obtained from 30 participants, with an average of 2,274 APP records per user. In the Application dataset, users employed a total of 1,030 different APPs, averaging 34.3 different APPs per participant. This result is lower than the research of Carrascal and Church (2015) (with an average of 53.6 different APPs per user).

We divided 1,030 different APPs into 24 types based on previous studies (Carrascal and Church, 2015) on the classification methods of APPs, combined with the classification categories in the APP stores of the Android Market. Table 3.1 lists the top 10 categories of APPs launched most frequently by participants, including the number of unique APPs under their category, and APP instances used the most in each type. In this section, we refer to the APP categories as "APP topics."

Table 3.1: Basic statistics of top 10 APPs				
APP Topic	Number of Launches	Percentage (%)	Number of Unique APPs	Examples
Mobile Management	193,174	18.87	139	Baidu Cloud, 360 Security
Mobile Tools	133,492	13.04	133	Google Input, Calendar
Social	117,317	11.46	11	WeChat, Mobile QQ
System and Settings	96,843	9.46	201	Settings, System Update
Message	76,881	7.51	37	Massage, Phone Call
Individual	55,076	5.38	28	Word Lock Screen, Travel Wallpaper
Q&A	45,760	4.47	31	Quora, Zhihu
Multimedia	43,201	4.22	56	KuGou, iQIYI
Office	34,908	3.41	34	Youdao Dict, WPS
Shopping	31,530	3.08	33	Taobao, Amazon

In addition, we referred to the concept of the "App Chain," proposed by Böhmer et al. (2011), which uses the 30-second division standard. That is, if there are not any data records within 30 s, subsequent occurrences of APP interactions will be attributed to the next "App Chain." In this study, we divided 120,102 APP chains, 52.24% of which only used a unique APP, followed by the use of two different APPs (22.49%); see Figure 3.1.

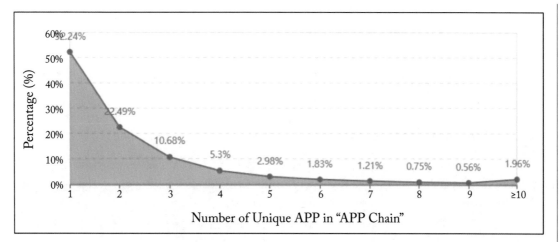

Figure 3.1: Statistics of users' App chain.

As shown in Figure 3.1, the lower number of unique APP in APP chain account for the highest proportion, indicating that users are more likely to use an APP for a long time when using a mobile phone, but this data is lower than the conclusion of Falaki et al. (2010).

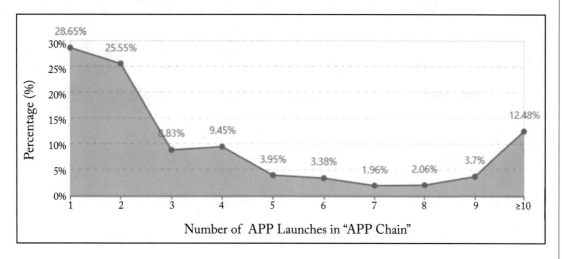

Figure 3.2: Statistics of APP launches in "App chain."

Figure 3.2 reflects the frequency distribution of the number of APP launches in an APP Chain. The proportion of APPs launched more than 3 times is 63.03%, followed by the proportion of APPs launched more than 10 times (12.5%). Combined with the interviews after the experiments, 28 participants expressed that they often interact with different APPs. Participant *P7* said,

"After using one APP, I will always start other APPs running in the background to browse." This reflects that, when using mobile phones, users will frequently interact with APPs.

3.1.2   THE RELATIONSHIP BETWEEN MOBILE SEARCH SESSIONS AND APP TOPICS

Interaction between Mobile Search Session and APP

In this section, a total of 2,875 queries were divided into 1,781 search sessions mentioned in Section 2.1.1. These search sessions included query content records and APP usage records without query submission.

Figure 3.3 reflects all the activities participant $P1$ did in a search session (S_{44}). He/she entered the query "Xiaosong Talk" (Q_{60}) via Sohu (a multimedia APP) at the beginning of the search session. He/she used WeChat, then launched the Baidu mobile browser, continuing to submit the query "Xiaosong Talk" (Q_{61}). After that, he/she opened the MIUI APP store and entered the query "Youku" (Q_{62}), then transitioned to WeChat again. By using the Youku APP and submitting the query "Xiaosong Talk" (Q_{63}) again, he/she used the APP for 2.5 min. Finally, he/she used the iQIYI APP to search for "Xiaosong Talk" (Q_{64}).

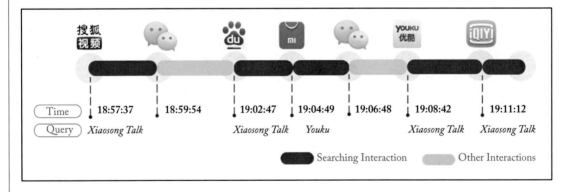

Figure 3.3: An instance of the APP interaction in the search session of participant $P1$.

Figure 3.3 reflects that a total of seven APP data records are included in this search session. The user used six different APPs, and, according to the previous classification of the APP type, these six APPs belong to four different APP topics. Affected by the diversity functions of the smartphone, especially the popularity of instant message APPs, users engaged in a variety of interactive activities in the mobile search process.

There was a total of 21,372 APP usage records in 1,781 search sessions, with 119 different APPs used. In each search session, users used 3.4 different APPs on average, including 12 APP records and 1.61 queries. This result is higher than the previous study by Church et al. (2008).

At the same time, in all search sessions, users used a total of 20 types of APPs, similar to the total number of APP topics in the experiment. In general, there are multiple APP records besides the query submitted in 97.53% of the search sessions, of which only 17.52% of the search sessions occurred in an APP, and in the other search sessions there were multiple records of APP interaction. Search sessions used two types of APPs 52% of the time.

The above data shows that the users' mobile search is often accompanied by other activities and is also susceptible to other APP interactions. Therefore, it is necessary to combine traditional query submitting, search topic, and search time with APP usages to comprehensively analyze search behavior.

Relation between Query and APP Usage

We studied APP usage when users submitted queries and found that 13 APP types were used in total to search for information. Table 3.2 lists the top 5 APP topics in the dataset. Results show that users used only 7 unique browsers and search APPs, but 46.12% of the queries are submitted through this type of APP, while 8.38% of the queries are submitted through 18 different multimedia APPs.

APP Topic	Number of Queries Submitted	Number of Unique APPs	Percentage (%)
Browser and Search Engine	1326	7	46.12
Office	490	12	17.04
Shopping	264	9	9.18
Multimedia	241	18	8.38
Mobile Management	173	16	6.02

Table 3.2: Top 5 APP topic when users submitted queries

After the experiment, we conducted user interviews regarding this phenomenon, in which participant *P2* explained the reason why he/she used seven different multimedia APPs to search: "Because I often do not know the copyright of the variety shows belongs to which platform, I often download a lot of APPs to see different videos." In addition, 14 participants said that they usually use the mobile browser APP that comes with their mobile phones, resulting in a smaller number of browse and search APPs.

In addition, participants used social APPs (4.52%), travel APPs (4.35%), lifestyle APPs (2.54%), finance APPs (0.9%), weather APPs (0.45%), reader APPs (0.38%), game APPs (0.07%), and tools APPs (0.03%) for mobile searching. Compared to desktop search, in which browsers are the main search method, there are abundant ways to search in the mobile setting.

3.1.3   THE RELATIONSHIP BETWEEN MOBILE INFORMATION NEEDS AND APP TOPICS

We discuss the relationship between the search time of the user's mobile search, the search topic, and the APP topics using the concept of Pointwise Mutual Information (PMI) (Zhu et al., 2012), a commonly used method in information theory and statistics that can be used to measure the relevance of two or more factors. Montañez et al. (2014) used it to evaluate the relationship between search topic, device, and search time. The formula is:

$$PMI\,(x;y) = log\ \frac{p(x,y)/}{p(x)p(y)} = log\ \frac{p(x|y)}{p(x)}\ .$$

When the PMI value is positive, it indicates that the relationship between the two factors is strong, while the negative value reflects the weak relations.

In our study, we chose the top 6 APP topics that were used to submit the queries and analyzed the relationship between these APP topics and the search topics by calculating the value of PMI (search topic, APP topic), as shown in Figure 3.4. When users searched for information on different topics, the distribution of PMI values is quite varied, reflecting the relationship between the specific topic information being searched for and certain types of APPs.

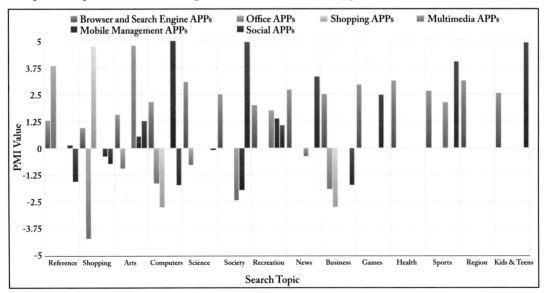

Figure 3.4: Analysis of the relevance of the search topic and the APP topic.

Based on the increasing popularity of specialty APPs, users' search topics tend to be consistent with APP topics. In this section, the proportion of specialty APP usage was 53.88%, the most obvious of which is that when users used office APPs, the relationship between the reference category information and office APPs is all positive, and the PMI value of office APPs and other search topics is all negative. When users search for computer information, such as searching for a mobile APP, they will use mobile management APPs more, with the highest PMI value of 4.962. When they search for arts information, the strongest relationship is shown with multimedia APPs, with PMI value of 4.744. As for shopping APPs, there is a clear and positive relationship with the search of shopping topic, with a PMI value of 4.717. These results reflect that when users search for reference, shopping, art, and computer information, they are more inclined to use professional specialty APPs.

On the other hand, when users search for certain topics of information, they might not gravitate toward the same type of APP (17.57%). The most obvious example is when users use the browser and search engine APPs and social APPs, there is no significant difference in distribution of different search topics. For example, when the users use the browser and search engine APPs, the PMI values of different types of search topics are all positive, showing a uniform distribution. There is an especially strong relationship between browser and specialty search engine APPs and the topics science, news, health, games, region, and sports, with PMI values greater than 2.5. This indicates that users could use browser and search engine APPs when searching for all topics of information. Additionally, there is relationship between the use of social APPs and many search topics. When searching for social, news, sports, kid, and teen information, users will prioritize social APPs. For example, user $P17$ mentioned in the interview, "when there is sudden news, I like to search on Sina Weibo (a social APPs in China), due to the update being faster."

Diversification of APPs provides users with richer search methods. However, there is a weak relationship between some search topics and APP topics. For example, the relationship between computer topics and shopping APPs is negative (PMI = -2.73). When users search for business information, the probability of using shopping APPs is low (PMI = -2.735), while the relationship with browser and search engine APPs is strong (PMI = 2.581). Combined with the queries users submitted, we found that when the user searched for business information, the use of browser and search engine APPs reaches 64.37%, while the use of finance APPs is only 28.89%. In addition, when users searched for news information, they preferred using social APPs over news APPs, which reflects a lack of search function in the news APPs.

Overall, in the mobile environment, users will be more inclined to use specialty APPs to search rather than browsers or search engines. The appearance of the specialty APPs and the improvement of in-app search functions make the users' selectable search channels more diversified, and they are more inclined to use specialty search APPs to obtain accurate and fast results and improve the search experience.

3.1.4   TEMPORAL FEATURES OVER APP TOPICS IN MOBILE SEARCH

Relationship between Search Time Duration and APP Topic

In this section, we analyze the search sessions including more than one query in the dataset, and then count the time duration between the different types of APPs after submitting queries, the results of which are shown in Figure 3.5. As shown, in the comparative complex search sessions, the difference of the average duration on different APPs is more obvious. In regard to browser and search engine APP usage, the mean time duration is the longest, and in the use of weather APPs, the mean time duration is the shortest.

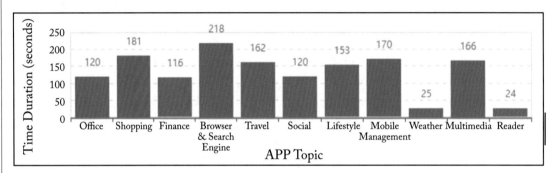

Figure 3.5: Average length of time users stayed on different APPs.

Because we could not record the user's clicks on URLs after submitting queries, we can only judge whether the user is satisfied with the search results by the length of time he/she stayed on an APP. A longer time duration on APPs without query submission can indicate a user's higher satisfaction with the search results.

At the same time, in a search session that contains multiple queries, the users could submit the queries via multiple APP interactions. In this section, we also account for the time duration on APPs when users submitted multiple queries in complex search sessions, the results of which are shown in Figure 3.6. In the previous study, we found that 89.22% of query input times are less than 10 s (Wu et al., 2016a). Combined with the time duration on the first APP in the search session shown in Figure 3.6, we can see that users will continue to use APPs after submitting queries instead of ending the search activity immediately. In addition, the time duration of users' interactions with APPs is longer at the beginning of a search session. User interaction with the first APP in a search session is the longest (average 204 s). Additionally, the time duration of interactions with APPs after the first in-search session would gradually reduce. Combined with the post-experiment interview, 90% of users expressed that they used a mobile phone to search for information that can be easily found, and they could find suitable results within one or two queries. Participant P14 said, "if I can't find useful results, I will not pay much attention to the result pages and I will consider using a computer to search."

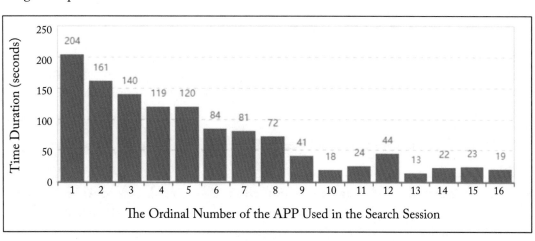

Figure 3.6: The average duration in APPs in the search sessions.

Relationship between Search Time Duration and Information Need

The web search query classification can reflect the user's information needs and interests. In Section 2.1.1, we classified all queries into 14 different search topics. Figure 3.7 reflects the mean time duration when users searched for different topics of information in search sessions that contain multiple queries.

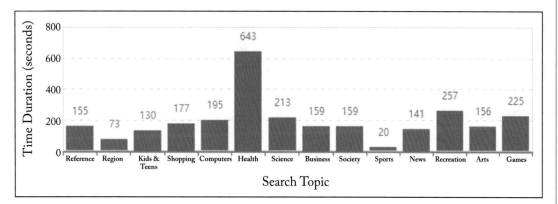

Figure 3.7: Average duration of mobile searches when searching for different topics.

When users search for health information, the mean time duration is 643 s. However, the proportion of this topic is not high in all queries. Thus, after the experiment, we interviewed the users who searched for this topic. Participant *P2* said, "I searched for some illnesses information because I felt uncomfortable, but the answer is not very clear, so I read a lot of online friends' answers." Participant *P21* expressed, "I searched for some drugs, then I did careful examination. Because it was related to health, so it took more time." The searches for sports, region, kids and teens, news, and other topics of information take less time.

As a result, according to the users' information needs, search motivations, and the level of urgency of the search tasks, the time duration on APPs would vary when searching for different topics of information.

Comprehensive Analysis of Search Topic, Search Time, and APP Topic

As mentioned earlier, the relationship between a user's search topic and the specialty APP used is not exactly a positive one. Understanding the time characters during the use of APPs in mobile search can help web information service providers understand the users' search preferences. They can optimize the network environment in the high frequency period of mobile searches to improve users' information search efficiency. Therefore, we factor time into the calculation process of PMI values, and the relationship between search topic and APP topic in different time dimensions will be explored.

Through the four subgraphs in Figure 3.8, we can see that searches about science on office APPs mainly occur at 3:00 am, 9:00 am, and 6:00 pm; the relationship between science topic searches and office APPs is strong at these time points, while the relationship between science topic searches and browser and search engine APPs is weak, and most PMI values are negative.

If users used social APPs to search for social information, there is a peak of PMI value at 6-7 am. The PMI value is also positive for other hours of the day. At the same hours, the situation in which users employ browser and search engine APPs to search for social information is just the opposite, with a negative PMI value and a weak relationship. This reflects that users prefer using particular types of APPs when they search for certain topics of information.

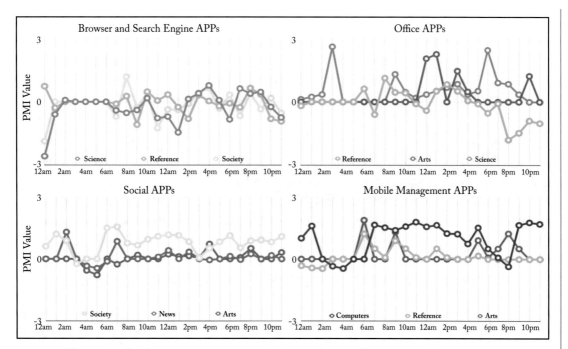

Figure 3.8: Association analysis of search topic, search time, and APP type

For searches about arts information, when users used office APPs and mobile management APPs, the time distribution varied. This indicates that the difference in APP topic used when searching for the same topic of information would also result in different time distribution characteristics.

Figure 3.8 reflects the time distribution when searching for the same topic of information on different types of APPs, which provides data to support an understanding of user preferences on various APPs.

Through the analysis above, we can conclude that the types of APPs used in mobile search could lead to a difference in search time duration. In complex search sessions, there is a large difference between time durations on different APPs. The mean time duration on browser and search engine APPs is longest, which is similar to previous studies (Böhmer et al., 2011). Overall, compared to general users (Falaki et al., 2010), college students are inclined to use one type of APP for a long time during a mobile search. Furthermore, the search topic also affects the distribution of the time duration.

3.2   APP TRANSITION IN MOBILE SEARCH

Mobile users also often multi task using several APPs at the same time. Furthermore, mobile users may resume a previous search after a long time. For example, a user searched an address on *Tencent*

Mobile Map, and after a short time, searched it again on *Baidu Mobile Map*. Therefore, we define the transitions between APPs as the process of usages from the first APP to the second APP. Research on APP transition, especially on the transition of APPs when users conduct a mobile search, can help to detect mobile search patterns and to analyze the context, motivation, strategy, and other factors in long search sessions. It can contribute to the interactive design of APPs, such as search and APP recommendations.

Consequently, transitions from one APP to another during users' mobile phone interactions are commonplace. Research from the perspective of search sessions can help to understand how users transition between APPs, and to detect the intent motivation behind these transitions. Therefore, we seek to understand the transitions between APPs in mobile search and focus on the probabilities, paths, and patterns during the APP transitions. We also discuss user intent in APP transitions.

3.2.1   APP TRANSITION PROBABILITIES BETWEEN MOBILE QUERIES

APP-APP Transition Probabilities

In this section, we focus on the APP-APP transition in the process of submitting queries based on the keyboard dataset. Self-transition is defined as the transitions between the same or different unique APPs belonging to the same types.

We calculated the probabilities of transitions in each search session, including the self-transition, as shown in Figure 3.9. The Y axis is the first type of APP used in the initial query, and the X axis is the subsequent type of APP used in the second query. The number and color of each cell in the figure represent the probabilities of APP-APP transition. The deeper the color of the cell, the higher the probability of transition. Cells without values indicate there were no transitions between two types of APPs during the query submission.

As seen in Figure 3.9, when participants used browser and search engine APPs in their first query, they were likely to use eight types of APPs in the second query. For mobile management APPs in the first query, the probable types of APPs used in the second query is seven.

The results also show that participants could choose particular APPs when searching for a specific topic, like finance APPs, weather APPs, game APPs, and reader APPs, so there were no transitions between these APPs and other types. Due to the rapid development of specialty APPs (e.g., shopping information from Taobao APP), the search results from these APPs could easily meet their needs.

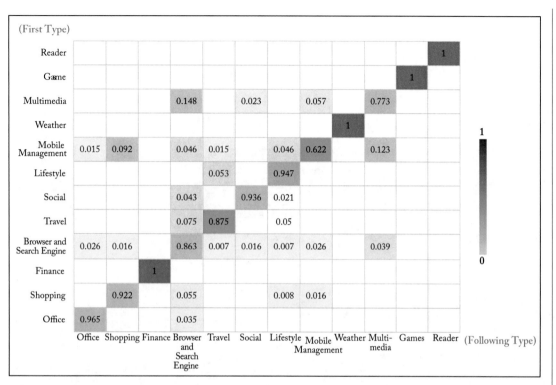

Figure 3.9: The probabilities of APP-APP transition.

Drawing from the qualitative data in the structured diaries, when participants' searches (30.38%) were "Part of success" and "Will continue search," they would use two or more APPs. Therefore, when participants decided to continue a search, they would prioritize the same APP or the same types of APPs. Especially if they searched for information about finance, games, and so on, they all switched to the same types of APPs.

Self-transition of the Same Type APP

As seen in Figure 3.9, the probabilities of self-transition are the highest, in that participants would give priority to the same type of APPs when deciding whether or not to continue searching. As participant P17 said in the interview, "I'd like to continue search on the same APP when I wanted to find better search results."

We found there were two features of self-transition. One was the use of the same unique APP, such as using Android Market in the first query and continuing to use it later for second query. Another was using different unique APPs belonging to the same type. For example, participant P14 submitted "MacBook" on Jingdong and then searched it on Mobile Suning (S_{1105}, Q_{1767}, and Q_{1768}), which were both shopping APPs. He explained, "I used two APPs mainly because that I wanted to know which was cheaper and whether there was discount on these two APPs."

The former feature reflects continued searching, while the latter feature reflects feedback and strategies of participants' mobile searches.

3.2.2   APP TRANSITION PATHS BETWEEN MOBILE QUERIES

To understand the relationship between different types of APPs in the process of mobile search, we eliminated self-transitions, which meant that the types of APPs used in the first query were different from those in the second query.

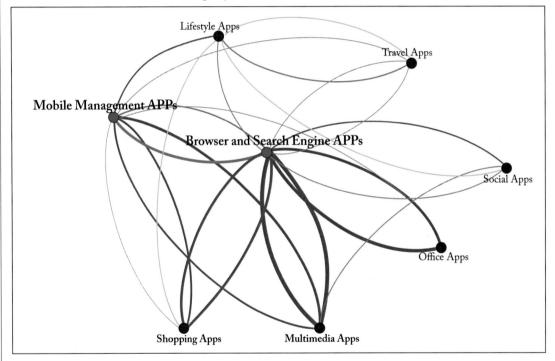

Figure 3.10: Probabilities of transition between different types of APPs

Figure 3.10 reflects the probabilities of transition between different types of APPs, excluding self-transition. The node represents the different types of APPs, and the line represents the exited transition between two APPs. Line thickness indicates the probabilities of transition, with thicker lines meaning a higher probability.

We found that there is a strong relationship between browser and search engine APPs and multimedia APPs. Participant $P26$ searched "Happy Camp" (S_{1645}, Q_{2656}) on *iQIYI*, and searched it again on *MGTV* (S_{1645}, Q_{2656}) because the second APP owned the copyright of this show. We found participants often submitted the same query on different types of APPs (103 queries).

Referring to the interview, we consider that this is mainly because of confusion and uncertainty surrounding copyrights of music, videos, etc. Some music and video sites in China, such as iQIYI, have monopolized many video resources, so users who do not know the owner of particular videos' copyrights could search again after unsuccessful searches through the browser and search engine APPs. These processes could trigger many transitions.

3.2.3   APP TRANSITION PATTERNS IN SEARCH SESSIONS

There were three stages when participants searched information: *Pre-query*, *Query*, and *Post-query*. Participants could submit query (Q_{i-1}) or not (non-query) before the query (Q_i), and the situation after Q_i was the same in the experiment. In each stage, participants used one APP, and there were four patterns (pattern I, pattern II, pattern III, pattern IV) of transitions about APP usages, as shown in Figure 3.11.

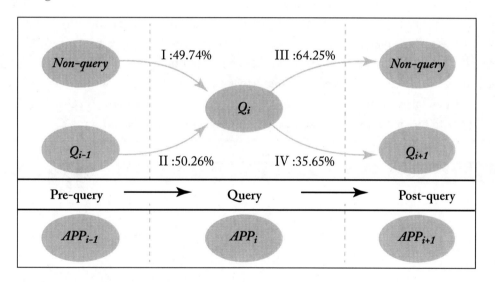

Figure 3.11: The pattern of APP-APP transition.

Results showed that in the transition from **Pre-query** to **Query**, the proportion of pattern I (non-query to Q_i) and pattern II (Q_{i-1}-1 to Q_i) is relatively similar, while in the transition from **Query** to **Post-query**, the difference between pattern III (Q_i to non-query) and pattern IV (Q_i to Q_{i+1}+1) is large. Previous work only proposes the lifecycle (installing, updating, uninstalling, opening, and closing the APP) of APP usages (Böhmer et al., 2011) without concentrating on the process of APP-APP transitions.

Table 3.3 presents the top 2 transitions between APPs in each pattern. In pattern I (non-query to Q_i), the most common transition is from instant communication APPs to browser and search engine APPs (31.03%), followed by from social APPs to browser and search engine APPs (19.36%). Based on the structured diaries, 54.63% participants chose the option of "chatting with friends or families on APPs," and participant P6 said in the interviews that "I often searched something interesting while I browsed the content of social network." Therefore, we recognize that social contexts will trigger the majority of mobile searches.

For pattern II (Q_{i-1}-1 to Q_i) and pattern IV (Q_i to Q_{i+1}+1), the most common transitions occur between the same type of APPs, such as from a mobile browser to itself. This indicates that if participants decide to continue searching, they prefer it be in the same APP or the same types of APPs.

As for the transition from **Query** to **Post-query**, the proportion of pattern III (Q_i to non-query) is much higher than pattern IV (Q_i to Q_{i+1}+1). In pattern III (Q_i to non-query), there are also common transitions from browser and search engine APPs to shopping APPs (5.36%) and social APPs (5.08%). In the interview, participant $P17$ said, "When I searched a song, my boyfriend sent a message to me, so I launched the Wechat to answer." We also found that there were 27 follow-up actions, such as making purchases and sharing search results after a query. Participant $P22$ searched for the date of a football event on *Android Browser* and shared the results on Mobile *QQ*. Through the structured diaries and interviews, we found that these follow-up actions were motivated by goal-oriented mobile searches. Therefore, we conclude that transition pattern III (Q_i to non-query) is mainly due to the interruption of mobile search and subsequent follow-up actions.

Table 3.3: Top 2 APP-APP transition in each pattern			
Pattern	**Type of First APP Used**	**Type of Second APP Used**	**Rate (%)**
I	instant communication	browser and search engine	31.03
	social	browser and search engine	19.36
II	browser and search engine	browser and search engine	26.12
	office	office	14.2
III	browser and search engine	browser and search engine	32.25
	browser and search engine	instant communication	15.68
IV	browser and search engine	browser and search engine	24.46
	office	office	15.82

Overall, we found that the pattern of non-query to Q_i (pattern I) often occurs before the searches, similar to the work of Carrascal and Church (2015) that suggests that users tend to start APP sessions with the intention of searching. The interaction with the social APPs and the social context will trigger the majority of mobile searches.

While the patterns Q_{i-1} to Q_i (pattern II) and Q_i to Q_{i+1} (pattern IV) happen among the adjacent queries in one search session, in general, these transitions occur between the same and different types of APPs; the former is called self-transition and accounted for the most. This reflects that users prefer using the same APPs to continue searching. Interestingly, when participants used mobile management APPs or multimedia APPs first, a higher proportion transferred to different types of APPs. Taking the search topic into consideration, when they searched information about finance and weather, there were few transitions.

After the searches, the pattern of Q_i to non-query (pattern III) occured most frequently, which proves that users could do other interactions like browsing, downloading, sharing, etc., instead of locking the screen.

3.2.4   APP TRANSITION INTENTS OF MOBILE SEARCH

As noted, APP transitions between the same types of APPs are called self-transition. If APP transitions occurred in the pattern of non-query to Q_i (pattern I), it always happened under social contexts and users' other APPs activities, such as chatting and browsing, which could trigger a mobile search.

The reasons for transition of pattern for Q_{i-1} to Q_i (pattern II) and pattern Q_i to Q_{i+1} (pattern IV) are activities for continued searching. The self-transitions were made up of transitions to the same types of APPs and to different and unique APPs of the same type. In these two patterns, individuals preferred the same APP or the same type of APPs and the probabilities of self-transition were the highest in the search sessions. On the contrary, the transitions to different types of APPs tended to occur because of dissatisfaction with the original search results. Especially for searches conducted on multimedia APPs, confusion and uncertainty about the copyrights of movies, videos, and other media triggered transitions.

If there are not subsequent queries, as in the pattern of Q_i to non-query (pattern III), the transitions to the same types of APPs often signal other activities, such as browsing. Our results also show that there are more transitions to APPs without query submissions, similar to previous research (Carrascal and Church, 2015). Based on the interviews and structured diaries, this pattern is mainly due to interruptions of the mobile search and follow-up actions after searching. Our results show that participants shared search results, made purchases, and so on through another APP, reflecting satisfaction with the search results.

3.3   FOLLOW-UP ACTIONS TRIGGERED BY MOBILE SEARCH

In the above analysis about users' mobile search, we found that many users did not stop using their mobile phones after a search; on the contrary, they would interact with different APPs after searching. Google and Nielsen (2013) focused on the conversion of mobile search, finding that 73% of mobile searches lead to follow-up actions, such as continuing a search, visiting a website, sharing information, visiting a store, shopping, calling, etc. These follow-up actions triggered by mobile search can contribute to the understanding of the relationship between mobile search and other actions, and the research can be applied to help search providers improve the recommendations of search results and enrich the connotations of search behavior. The analysis of this section is based on the Experiment I, mentioned in the Section 1.4.

3.3.1   CATEGORY AND IDENTIFICATION OF FOLLOW-UP ACTIONS

In our study, most participants said in the interview that they would carry out follow-up actions within one day. Therefore, we defined actions after an initial search session within 24 hours as the follow-up actions triggered by a mobile search, such as making a purchase after searching for food. Due to user privacy protection and limitations of AWARE, we cannot identify other actions such as making phone calls, navigating a route, visiting certain places, and so forth.

We identified three categories of follow-up activities in this study. Figure 3.12 shows the examples of continuing search, making purchases, and sharing information.

Continuing Searching

According to the definition of the search session in Section 2.1.1, we define the continuing search as the action where a participant submitted one or more search sessions after the initial search session. We identified 179 continuing searches (86.89%). These queries might constitute several subsequent search sessions. Two methods below were used for identification..

(i) Co-occurrence of Unique Controlled Vocabularies

We found that the participants would search for relevant information after the initial search session, so we explored the relationship between search sessions to determine the follow-up actions of continuing search. "Co-occurrence" is an effective way to explore the relationship between two different search sessions. We mapped all queries to the controlled vocabularies or their super-verbs by the "Chinese Classified Thesaurus" (CCT), and deleted duplicate controlled vocabulary terms in each search session. If there were more than two of the same controlled vocabulary terms in the subsequent search session and the initial search session, it was considered to be a continuing search. As shown in Figure 3.12a, there are two co-occurrences of unique controlled vocabularies between S_{841} and S_{842}. That is, S_{842} is a follow-up action of the continuing search triggered by S_{841}.

(ii) Recurrence of Query

In the dataset, we also found that the participants submitted the same query after the initial search session within 24 h, and in some cases they used the same APP to search. This mobile search with recurrence of query in the subsequent search session is also considered to be a continuing search. In our dataset, 23 instances of continuing search belong to this type.

P_i	S_i	Q_i	Time	APP	Query/ Current_text	Controlled Vocabularies	Unique Controlled Vocabularies in Each Search Session
P_{11}	S_{841}	Q_{1349}	17:16:10	Xiaomi APP Store	MUI	Mobile phone, operataion system	Mobile phone, operataion system, mobile software
		Q_{1350}	17:17:35	Android Browser	MUI root APP	Mobile phone, operataion system, mobile	
P_{11}	S_{842}	Q_{1351}	17:35:27	Android Browser	MUI root caution	Mobile phone, operataion system	Mobile phone, operataion system

(a) The example of Continuing Searching

P_i	S_i	Q_i	Time	APP	Query/ Current_text
P_5	S_{312}	Q_{514}	9:34:10	ele.me	Pan pizza
	/	/	9:35:38	ele.me	"I prefer tomato paste, please help me to put some more, thank you"

(b) The example of Making a Purchase

P_i	S_i	Q_i	Time	APP	Query/ Current_text
P_{28}	S_{1686}	Q_{2732}	7:48:31	Android Browser	Lecture on cross culture
		Q_{2733}	7:51:05	Sina Weibo	Lecture on cross culture
	/	/	8:03:04	Sina Weibo	"#Lecture on cross culture#The lecture will begin on 5pm at 301"

(c) The example of Sharing Information

Figure 3.12: The example of follow-up actions. Note: The "/" in the figure means that the log data record without query submission.

Making Purchase

Making a purchase (5.83%) is the action of buying goods after the initial search session, as shown in Figure 3.12b. We confirmed that participants made a purchase after the initial search session through payment records from APPs, purchase orders, notes on shopping APPs and the content from the structured diary and interview. Participant P5 said in the interview that he searched for two stocks that he was interested in by entering the stock code (S_{341}, Q_{577}, and Q_{578}) through Mobile Baidu and then made a decision to buy the stock ICBC in 13 min. The amount of purchases is similar to the Google, IpsosMediaCT, and Purchased's (2014) study on American users (7%). All purchases made during the experiment were via mobile shopping. This result reflects that e-commerce and electronic payment offer convenience for college students. It is absolutely true that participants might visit the store after a mobile search, but we were not able to record those actions.

We also found that participants made purchases after comparing different search results. This enables some applications (for example, the shopping APPs) to provide convenient services for users to compare different information and improve efficiency

Sharing Information

The phenomenon of sharing information on the Web, especially misinformation (Church et al., 2008), has been studied. Sharing information in this work is the action of sharing search results to participants' social networks through APPs after conducting a mobile search, as seen in Figure 3.12c. The proportion of sharing information in our study (7.28%) is lower than Neustar's research (18%) (2014). Similar to making purchases, all sharing information was online only; therefore we could not record word-of-mouth sharing actions.

This reveals that search engines that can help users share more complex results by including more convenient methods to optimize the search experience.

3.3.2   TEMPORAL FEATURES OF FOLLOW-UP ACTIONS

We analyzed the time interval between the initial search session and follow-up actions. The time interval is the time difference between the start of follow-up actions and the end of initial search sessions. In our dataset, the follow-ups like making purchases and sharing information were all triggered by one search session, while continuing search (26.26%) was composed of two or more subsequent search sessions. For these continuing searches with several subsessions, we counted the time interval using the sum of each time interval among subsessions and divided by the number of subsessions.

The results show that the average time interval for continuing search is 2 h and 46 min, while the average value for making purchases (13 min) and sharing information (6 min) is shorter. The shortest time interval is only 15 s, whereas the longest is close to 15 h. We found that actions with time intervals of more than 2 h because of a temporary interruption had "less urgent" information needs.

We analyzed the follow-up actions whose time intervals were more than 1 h, finding that these actions were mainly triggered by information needs for Recreation. It was often about future plans or arrangements, and not something they needed immediately.

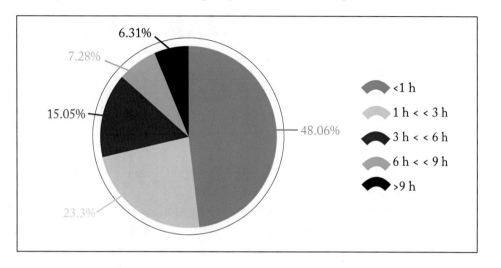

Figure 3.13: Time interval of follow-up actions.

In general, the vast majority of follow-up actions (48.06%) occurred within 1 h, and 41.34% of follow-ups of continuing search occurred within 1 h, both of which are less than Google and Nielsen's research (2013). The follow-ups for making purchases and sharing information were all triggered within 1 h, higher than Google and Nielsen's research (2013).

3.3.3   FOLLOW-UP ACTIONS TRIGGERED BY INFORMATION NEEDS

In order to understand what category of information searched for by the participants would trigger follow-up actions, we used the classification of information needs from Section 2.2.1 to classify the needs of each initial search session into 12 primary categories and the respective subordinate categories.

Results showed that the needs for Reference (26.21%), Shopping (17.48%), Computers (11.65%), and Arts (9.22%) triggered the majority of follow-up actions, followed by Society (7.28%), Science (6.8%), and Recreation (5.83%), as shown in Figure 3.14.

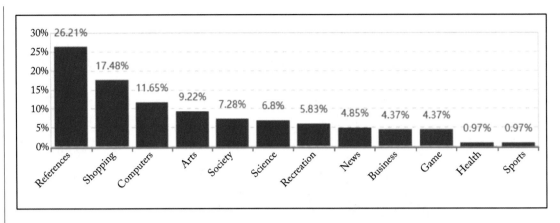

Figure 3.14: Time interval of follow-up actions.

The follow-up actions of making purchases were mainly triggered by the need for Food (58.33%). This was largely due to the convenience of takeout food services; as participant P5 said, "I preferred searching for takeout food because it was convenient."

Participants with different information needs could trigger sharing information actions, such as Society, Science, Reference, Recreation, Computers, News, Health, Arts, etc. When participants chatted with others via mobile phone, the search activities that occurred in this period led to sharing information more easily.

As continuing search accounts for most, if not all, of the follow-up actions, we discuss the main reasons behind it. The first is that participants continued the same search task to a deeper level after the initial session by modifying the queries in subsequent search sessions. For example, participant $P7$ searched, "Can I return the alternative train ticket?" (S_{380}). Due to disappointing results, he continued to submit, "Can I return the alternative train ticket immediately by 12306?" (S_{381}). This reflects a clarification of information need.

The second reason is that participants searched for information related to the initial search session or searched for something inspired by new information needs. For example, participant $P7$ searched "feature spot in Suzhou" and "Humble Administrator's garden" (S_{460}, Q_{746}, and Q_{747}). After 55 min, he continued searching other featured spots like "Suzhou's moat" and "Songhe Building of Suzhou"(S_{461}, Q_{748}, and Q_{749}). Participant $P13$ had searched for information about Recreation in the initial search session, while searching other information about Reference, like maps, later.

The third reason is repeated searching, as described in Section 3.3.1. Participants' search process might be interrupted for some reason. Participant $P4$ said in the interview, "I wanted to know whether the China Post on the Bayi Road exist (S_{371}) but was interrupted by my friends, so

I searched it later (S_{373})." Furthermore, they would use other APPs to submit the same query as a result of dissatisfaction with the initial search results.

3.3.4 THE RELATIONSHIP BETWEEN APP TRANSITIONS AND FOLLOW-UP ACTIONS

In Section 3.2, we studied the phenomenon of APP transitions in mobile search. In the analysis of follow-up actions, we found that participants often used different APPs in the 62 follow-up actions. All sharing information occurred through different APPs, while 21.79% of continuing search and 66.67% of making purchases used different APPs.

We also found that if the participants used search engine APPs (34.65%) in the initial search sessions, they were more prone to using different APPs later, followed by shopping APPs with 18.81%.

APP transitions in follow-up actions can be divided into two cases. One is using the same type of unique APP, such as Twitter and Facebook. We found that participants used the same type of different APPs in 19 follow-up actions. The other is using different types of APPs. For instance, participant $P22$ used a mobile search engine APP to search for a current event about "Lin Senhao's death," and then used the Mobile QQ to share the information with his friend.

We use "A→B" to represent using different types of APPs in follow-up actions. The data shows that "search engine APPs→social APPs" and "shopping APPs→search engine APPs" appear the most. If participants filled in "not entirely successful" or "failure" about a search, and said, "I'm willing to continue searching" in the structured diary, the probability of using different APPs in the follow-up actions was high.

Overall, smartphones, tablets, and other mobile devices have the advantages of mobility, portability, and speed. As a result, the use of mobile search for college students is growing rapidly. Compared to computer and other desktop devices, mobile devices play more of a role in college students' daily life and learning. They search more categories of information on mobile devices. Their needs' distribution reflects the content of daily life of college students to a certain extent, and also reflects the high-frequency use of the mobile phone. There are more types of mobile search follow-up actions than those of desktop searches because of mobile phones' mobility, portability, and speed. The use of mobile phones may trigger more follow-up actions than the desktop.

3.4 SUMMARY

This chapter summarizes the objective data of how college students in real life use their mobile phones, as demonstrated in Experiment I. The APP types employed by the users in this experiment to submit queries were organized and analyzed from the perspective of the search session to explore the users' complex search behavior. At the same time, the causes of user behavior were investigated through interviews after the experiment. Through calculating the relevance of influencing factors and analyzing the cross effects among search topics, search time, and types of APPs used by the user in the mobile environment, it was found that users searching for shopping information and so on were more biased toward specialty search engines, while they were not limited to use of one type of APP on health classes, science classes, and other information searches. When searching for information of the same topic type, search time also affected the use of the APP.

In view of the characteristics of users' mobile search behaviors, specialty search engines should provide better search services. Internet enterprises should try to integrate APP ecosystems and search entrances, and combine these with users' search habits to provide initiative information recommendation services.

In our analysis about mobile search and APP usage, we found that users interact multiple times with APPs during the mobile search process. Therefore, we analyzed APP usages while performing mobile search and the transitions in mobile search. We proposed four transition patterns and found that self-transition occurs the most. Before the search, interactions with communication APPs and a social context could trigger most searches, while there are more actions without queries after searches. Combined with the qualitative study, we believed that the causes of APP-APP transition are mainly due to the feedback from search results, interruptions while searching, and the follow-up actions after searches.

In the users' APP transition behaviors, some were engaged in other activities related to the mobile search. We refer to these activities as follow-up actions triggered by the mobile search. We classified the follow-up actions triggered by college students' mobile search, such as continuing search, making purchases, and sharing information, and introduced the definition and identification criteria for these follow-up actions. We studied the characteristics and discussed the causes of these follow-up actions.

Interestingly, there is a close connection between follow-up actions and information needs. The participants' information needs could change during the follow-up actions in a search task. Follow-up actions triggered within 1 h of the initial search mainly were goal-oriented, and we can consider these actions as the purpose of the mobile searches as well.. Furthermore, participants might use another APP or several different APPs in the follow-up actions, primarily because the search results failed to meet participants' information needs, participants compared different search results, or they moved onto other activities due to satisfaction with the search results.

Through the analysis of the dataset, structured diaries, and interviews, we think that feedback from the search results is the main cause of follow-up actions. If users are satisfied with the search results, they may share information or make purchases immediately after searching. Otherwise, they will continue searching via different APPs or by modifying their queries.

CHAPTER 4

Mobile Search Behavior Across Different Devices

The widespread popularity of smartphones provides more options for users. When they need to access the Internet, they can use mobile phones, desktops, laptops, and tablets to search for online information. Device transition, the behavior of changing devices when searching, is an indispensable feature of cross-device search. In our book, a cross-device transition implies the existence of "pre-transition" and "post-transition" periods. A device can be either "pre-device" or the "post-device."

In this chapter, we mainly focus on the user's information preparation behavior, information resumption behavior, on-the-spot search performance, and predicting search performance in cross-device search context. The analysis of this chapter is based on the data from Experiment II in Section 1.4.

4.1 INFORMATION PREPARATION BEHAVIOR IN CROSS-DEVICE SEARCH

In the multi-device environment, a tourist who is planning a trip may search for introductions to historical sites through a laptop before he/she sets out. Then the mobile phone is used to search again for address information to help him/her get there. Alternatively, a Game of Thrones (GoT) fan is told about a plot leak when out for dinner and he/she looks up the news on a mobile phone. He/she may seek out the news in detail on the computer after arriving home. In both these cases, the transition between different devices interrupts the search task and the user has to resume repeated searching. If the post-transition session is regarded as resumption, the pre-transition device session can be seen as preparation. In this section, we discuss the search behavior in the preparation session of a cross-device search. We aim to understand what important features describe information preparation behavior, and to understand how the features characterize information preparation behavior.

4.1.1 DEFINITION OF INFORMATION PREPARATION

Session

The concept of a search session is employed to segment queries and associated search behaviors into short-time units for analysis. A threshold time is used to segment sessions in previous log analysis. However, in this chapter, we define a session from the perspective of device. Each cross-device search consists of two sessions: the pre-transition (Session 1) and post-transition session (Session 2).

Cross-device Search Task

A cross-device search is defined by Y. Wang et al. (2013) as a combination of an anterior device, a posterior device, a pre-transition session, a post-transition session and queries in both sessions. Based on this, we have defined the cross-device search in Section 1.2.5.

Information Preparation

Under the cross-device search context, users tend to repeat search tasks in a post-transition session; we consider their performance in a pre-transition session as the preparation for the task. Thus, given a cross-device search where repeated searches occur, information preparation refers to the search behaviors before transitioning to a different device.

4.1.2 MODELING INFORMATION PREPARATION BEHAVIOR

Identifying Information Preparation Behaviors

Since repeated searches indicate resumption, and the purpose of information preparation behaviors is to resume the search, we identify whether information preparation behaviors exist by whether there is repeated search in the cross-device search. Questionnaire results of Session 1 and Session 2 tell what subtasks the participant searched. We consider the participant to be performing information preparation if there is any subtask repeatedly searched. Table 4.1 shows the distribution of repeated searches. Over 90% of participants exhibited information preparation behaviors; specifically, 30 participants repeated the search of the first task and 32 participants repeated the second task.

Table 4.1: The number of users who repeatedly search the task

Repeated Subtask Number	0	1	2	3	4
The First Task	4	13	8	3	6
The Second Task	2	13	8	7	4
Percentage	8.8%	38.2%	23.5%	14.7%	14.7%

Features

We extracted features of query-based, click-based, time-based, and subjective evaluation groups from logs and questionnaire results, and these are described in more detail below (shown in Table 4.2). These features are used to train the model and can contribute to model information preparation and information resumption behavior, which will be mentioned in Section 4.2.2.

Table 4.2: Features for modeling the information preparation behavior	
Query-Based Features	
Query number	The number of queries.
Unique query number	The number of unique queries.
Query char	The number of characters in the query.
Unique query char	The number of characters of unique queries in the query.
Query term	The number of terms in the query.
Ave ED	The average length of Levenshtein edit distance of queries in the session.
Jaccard distance	The length of Jaccard distance between sessions in the task.
Click-Based Features	
Valid click rate	The frequency of clicks within result areas in the session.
Valid query rate	The frequency of clicks within result areas per query in the session.
Satisfied click rate	The frequency of clicks with landing page time of at least 30 s in the session.
Dissatisfied click rate	The frequency of clicks with landing page time of at most 15 s in the session.
Time-Based Features	
First click time	The interval of the first action and the first click in the session.
First valid click time	The interval of the first action and the first click within result areas in the session.
SERP time	The length of dwell time on SERPs in the session.
Landing page time	The length of dwell time on landing pages in the session.
Session time	The length of time that the session lasts.
Subjective Evaluation Features	
Satisfaction scores	The average scores to evaluate the satisfaction of the search.
Familiarity scores	The average scores to evaluate the familiarity of the task.

Query-based features describe the features of characters and terms in queries. Features associated with queries are used to predict the re-finding behavior (Tyler et al., 2010), and information preparation behavior is associated with re-finding. Thus, query-based features are important to model information preparation behavior.

Click-based features aim to capture the clicking behavior during information preparation. The concept of "valid click" derives from the result click (Guo and Agichtein, 2010), referring to the clicks on the result area as in Figures 1.9 and 1.10. Clicking the result area means the user takes advantage of the result information. The concepts of satisfied and dissatisfied clicks are defined by the dwell time on the landing page; 30 s and 15 s have been used as thresholds in previous research (Guo and Agichtein, 2010; Sculley et al., 2009). These click-based features reveal how much effort is required for information preparation.

Time-based features characterize information preparation behavior from the perspective of time length. Time can reflect the efficiency of information preparation. The user experiment offers users 20 min to search; however, effective searchers spend less time than that. A user clicks when he or she thinks the result is related to the task. Therefore, the time it takes to execute a click illustrates the speed of the relevance judgment and the focus of attention. Users stay on SERPs to scan results, while they remain on landing pages to acquire knowledge. The dwell time of SERPs and landing pages indicates the efficiency of information selection and information utilization.

The above features' groups are extracted from logs, while subjective evaluation features originate from the questionnaire survey. Scores of satisfaction and familiarity aim to capture subjective feelings about information preparation.

Classifiers

Three classifiers that were experimented with to model information preparation behavior were Binary Logistic Regression (BLR), C5.0 Decision Tree (C5.0), and Support Vector Machine (SVM). Logistic Regression is applied to predict task resumption by Kotov et al. (2011). Since information preparation is associated with resuming a task, the Binary Logistic Regression can be used to train the model. We refer to this classifier as a baseline, which was used the same way in Agichtein et al. (2012). Decision trees are effective for search behavior modeling, as shown in Tyler et al. (2010). It is easy to see what makes up the information preparation behavior by the structure of the tree. The Support Vector Machine shows its advantage on binary classification problems, although it is difficult for a model learned from it to explain the behavior. We ran these machine learning algorithms with IBM SPSS Modeler 18.

Dataset

It was mentioned in Section 4.1.2 that there are many more participants who performed information preparation behaviors than those who did not. Therefore, we balanced the positive and negative samples of all 68 sessions by way of random oversampling. The size of negative samples was increased by three times and finally we obtained 80 sessions for modeling. Among these, 70% of the sessions were used to train the model and the remaining 30% were used as the testing dataset. In order to overcome the overfitting problem of the small sample size, five-fold cross validation was applied when training the model. The results of modeling are discussed in the next section.

Results of Model Evaluation

The performance of three machine learning methods is compared using evaluation metrics of precision, recall, accuracy, and F1-score. Modeling results for whether the user performs information preparation in the cross-device search task in the training and testing datasets are presented in Table 4.3. It can be seen from the training dataset that the C5.0 Decision Tree predicts as well as the baseline, but Support Vector Machine performs a little worse. From the testing dataset, both the C5.0 Decision Tree and Support Vector Machine outperformed the baseline, and the C5.0 Decision Tree presents the best performance. Meanwhile, results show the prediction of null by both the baseline and Support Vector Machine, but not by the C5.0 Decision Tree, which indicates better performance of the latter. Considering the evaluation results and the interpretability, we gain insight into the information preparation behavior model by examining the structure of the C5.0 Decision Tree model.

Table 4.3: Evaluation results for model training by three classifiers

Dataset	Training			Testing		
Classifier	BLR (baseline)	C5.0	SVM	BLR (baseline)	C5.0	SVM
TP	41	42	33	15	17	14
FP	0	0	5	0	0	1
TN	13	13	8	5	5	4
FN	0	0	2	4	3	3
Precision	100.00%	100.00%	86.84%	100.00%	100.00%	93.33%
Recall	100.00%	100.00%	94.29%	78.95%	85.00%	82.35%
Accuracy	100.00%	100.00%	85.42%	83.33%	88.00%	81.82%
F1	100.00%	100.00%	90.41%	88.24%	91.89%	87.50%

4.1.3   UNDERSTANDING THE INFORMATION PREPARATION BEHAVIOR MODEL

Overview of the Model

Figure 4.1 shows the tree structure of the information preparation behavior model. We labeled the session with yes or no, based on whether the participant performed information preparation behaviors. Three rules based on the C5.0 Decision Tree and regarding the information preparation behavior are presented. First, list instances when the dissatisfied click rate of information preparation is no more than 0.636. Second, when the dissatisfied click rate is over 0.636, then the valid click rate is no more than 0.467 and the first valid click time is over 13610 ms. Finally, when the dissatisfied click rate is over 0.636, the valid click rate is no more than 0.467 and the first valid click time is no more than 13610 ms, then the Jaccard distance is no more than 0.778 and the satisfied click rate is no more than 0.114.

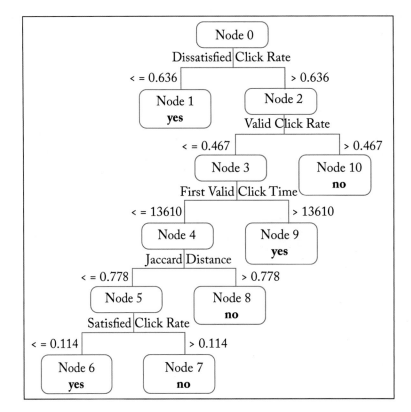

Figure 4.1: Information preparation behavior model.

The high dissatisfied click rate (<=0.636) and the low satisfied click rate (<=0.114) indicate search results cannot meet users' information need during information preparation of cross-device searches. Clicks within result areas witness a low frequency (<=0.467), meaning users of information preparation cannot easily find results relevant to their search task. The interval between the beginning of a search and the first valid click during the information preparation is at least 14 s. In other words, users of information preparation spend over 14 s determining result relevance. The Jaccard distance of queries in pre- and post-transition sessions is quite high (<=0.778), which illustrates the distinctive queries of information preparation.

Feature Analysis

There are five features included in the information preparation behavior model. The importance of these features is calculated by SPSS Modeler based on the following equation:

$$importance_i = \frac{1 - p_i}{\sum_i (1 - p_i)},$$

in which p refers to the p-value of F-Test. The higher the p-value is, the more likely the feature is correlated with the information preparation behavior. Figure 4.2 compares the importance of features. The most important feature is dissatisfied click rate, followed by first valid click time. Features of valid click rate, satisfied click rate, and Jaccard distance contribute less to the information preparation behavior model. We explore the five features in depth in what follows, based on data of those who conducted information preparation.

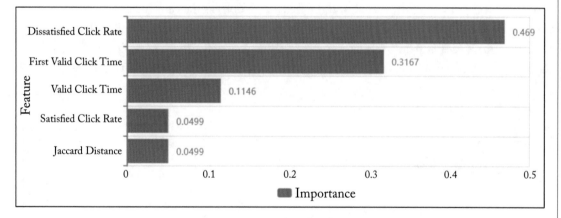

Figure 4.2: Importance of features in the information preparation behavior model.

(i) Dissatisfied Click Rate and Satisfied Click Rate

Distribution of the dissatisfied and satisfied click rates is shown in Table 4.4. Comparing the average and median reveals that dissatisfied click rate is a little higher than satisfied click rate; however, the standard deviations of these two features are similar. The result of Levene's Test illustrates the equal variances of two features and the T-test result indicates a significant difference. The number of dissatisfied clicks is significantly higher than that of satisfied clicks, which entices users to search the same task again on another device.

Table 4.4: Distribution of satisfied and dissatisfied click rate

Feature	Satisfied Click Rate	Dissatisfied Click Rate
AVE	0.36	0.49
MED	0.32	0.51
SD	0.25	0.26
F(sig.)	0.46	
t(sig.)	0.00	

(ii) First Valid Click Time

The length of time taken to execute the first click within result areas varies significantly, with about 2 s being the shortest length of time and 19 min the longest. We compare the distribution of first valid click time and first click as presented in Figure 4.3. Both types of clicks mainly occur within 1 min from the beginning of the search, and the frequency drops as the time increases. The frequency of the first valid click is less than that of the first click within 1 min, then exceeding the first click when the time is greater than 1 min. A significant difference of distributions of first valid click time and first click time is concluded by sig.=0.01 of Levene's Test and sig.=0.03 of T-test.

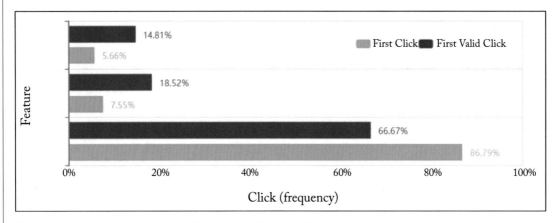

Figure 4.3: Contrast of first valid click time and first click time.

(iii) Valid Click Rate

Clicking within result areas can be considered a useful and effective search behavior. The average valid click rate is 0.55, with the standard deviation of 0.27, implying a better than average level of search performance during information preparation. We further investigate the distribution of valid clicks in a session lasting 20 min. It is found that valid clicks focus on three periods of a session, which are the very beginning, middle back, and near end of a session. K-means clustering method is applied to find the specific time of three focusing periods, and results show three cluster centers are 2, 9, and 16 min, respectively (see Table 4.5).

Table 4.5: Clustering valid clicks in a session

Cluster	Center/time	Item Number
1	2.46	153
2	16.17	164
3	9.41	132

.

(iv) Jaccard Distance

This feature describes the similarity of queries between the pre- and post-transition sessions. The feature of Levenshtein edit distance illustrates query similarity from a character perspective, while Jaccard distance is from the perspective of query terms. However, Jaccard distance is the one that is included in the information preparation behavior model. Hence, we assume that the characteristic of query term plays a more essential role in information preparation behavior. The average Jaccard distance is 0.71 and the amount of users with Jaccard distance over 0.5 accounts for 89%. A conclusion can be drawn that information preparation queries are greatly distinguished from queries used to repeat a search.

4.2   INFORMATION RESUMPTION BEHAVIOR IN CROSS-DEVICE SEARCH

The multi-device environment provides convenience for cross-device search activities. To complete a cross-device search task, device transition cannot be avoided and interrupts the continuation of the task. Researchers have found that users often need to remember the information searched in the pre-transition session in order to resume a task after an interruption (Teevan et al., 2007). In Section 4.1, we analyzed the information preparation behaviors in cross-device search. In this section, it is important to understand how people search to resume a task in the post-transition session, which we define as information resumption behaviors. We focus on the continuous task in cross-device web search and contribute to describing characteristics of information resumption behaviors. In addition, we intend to develop a model of information resumption behavior that focuses on the post-transition session of a cross-device search.

4.2.1   DEFINITION OF INFORMATION RESUMPTION

As mentioned in Section 4.1.1, the search session in this experiment was segmented by the device type. Furthermore, a search task consists of two search sessions. We provide a unified term and definition below.

- **Session 1** (similarly, pre-transition search session) is the first search session of a search task using one device.

- **Session 2** (similarly, post-switch search session) is the second search session of a search task using another device.

- **Query stream** includes all of the issued queries in a search session.

- **Valid click** means user's click occurred in the result area of SERP (except the blank area, top bar, out of bounds).

- **Information resumption behaviors** indicate user behaviors, including querying, clicking, cognition etc., in Session 2, only if the user resume the task by repeated searches.

4.2.2   MODELING INFORMATION RESUMPTION BEHAVIOR

Identifying the Information Resumption Behavior

In Experiment II, the questionnaire of Session 1 and Session 2 separately recorded the subtasks that the user searched in Session 1 and Session 2. Consequently, comparing records of the questionnaire and identifying repeated subtasks between Session 1 and Session 2, we made a judgment whether the user had information resumption behaviors in a cross-device search. The result is shown in Table 4.1 with over 90% participants exhibiting information resumption behaviors. Since information resumption behaviors are defined as search behaviors in Session 2, we then extracted features of information resumption behaviors from the behavior data collected in Session 2. Based on the questionnaire results, we labeled every Session 2 "yes" as having information resumption behaviors and "no" as not having information resumption behaviors.

Features

In this section, we analyze features that characterize information resumption behaviors. We present the information resumption behaviors by features of query, click, time, and context groups, collected from the logs and questionnaires of Session 2. The features used to model information resumption behaviors are shown in Table 4.2.

(i) Query Group

Research on query characteristics, such as query number, query length and so on, presents important aspects of querying behavior. A previous study found repeated queries after the interruption of a continuous task (Teevan et al., 2007; Han et al., 2015a), which shows that query-related features can be used to characterize information resumption behavior. In total, participants submitted 484 queries in Session 2, 359 of which are unique. The average query character length is 12.01. In addition, methods of calculating text similarity, e.g., Levenshtein edit distance and Jaccard similarity coefficient, can be used to reveal the relationship between behaviors in the pre- and post-transition sessions. In our data, the average Levenshtein edit distance of querying during information resumption is 6.41, and the average Jaccard similarity coefficient is 0.28 between Session 1 and Session 2. The average effective rate of one query is considered when analyzing the quality of querying during information resumption. Users click results after a query is submitted and the clicking behavior indicate that users may obtain useful information for their information need.

(ii) Click Group

These features aim to capture the level of task engagement during information resumption. The areas of SERP are labeled as shown in Figures 1.9 and 1.10. The concept of valid click derives from the result click (Guo and Agichtein, 2010), referring to clicks within the result area. There are 561 valid clicks from all participants in Session 2. The dwell time on the landing pages objectively reflects the degree of satisfaction with the results. We identified the satisfied click by a dwell time of more than 30 s (Fox et al., 2005) and dissatisfied click by a dwell time of less than 15 s (Sculley et al., 2009), which accounts for, respectively, 22.68% and 66.61% in Session 2.

(iii) Time Group

Users typically search for information in the following steps: issuing the query, browsing the SERP, clicking results, the landing page popping up, examining the landing page, returning to the SERP, and carrying on browsing. In this procedure, previous re-finding behavior studies show that results clicked toward the end of a session were more likely to be re-found during a later session than clicks made at the beginning, while re-finding was more likely to happen at the beginning of the later session than at the end (Tyler et al., 2010). This suggests that time can reflect the efficiency of information resumption. The dwell time of SERPs indicates the speed of browsing the results and relevance judgment, and landing page time indicates the usefulness of the result. According to our statistics, the average dwell time of SERPs is 9.45 minutes and the average examining time of landing pages is 8.69 minutes in Session 2.

(iv) Context Group

Unlike the above three feature groups collected based on the logs, this feature group comes from the questionnaire that was used to collect the data of cognition by a 5-point Likert scale. Scores of satisfaction and familiarity were calculated to capture subjective feelings about information resumption.

Classifiers

In this section, three modeling methods, Binary Logistic Regression (BLR), C5.0 Decision Tree (C5.0), and Support Vector Machine (SVM), were used. Logistic Regression (LR) has been used to predict search task continuation (Kotov et al., 2011; Agichtein et al., 2012). Since the information resumption behavior occurs along with task resumption or continuation, Binary Logistic Regression can be used to train the model. We refer to this classifier as a baseline, which was used the same way in Kotov et al. (2011). As mentioned in Tyler et al. (2010), the model trained by the Decision Tree is easy to interpret, meaning that by looking at the structure of the tree, one can gain an understanding of what makes up the behavior. In the Decision Tree model, each child branch can effectively be considered an independent model to explain information resumption behaviors. The Support Vector Machine has its own advantage regarding classification problems. We ran these machine-learning algorithms with IBM SPSS Modeler 18. Since our dataset is imbalanced between users who had information resumption behaviors and others who did not, we balanced the dataset in order to improve the accuracy of training as mentioned in Section 4.1.2. Among all sessions of the dataset, the ratio between the training set and the testing set was 7:3 and we performed 5-fold cross validation to avoid the overfitting problem.

4.2.3 UNDERSTANDING INFORMATION RESUMPTION BEHAVIOR

Comparing the Prediction Methods

To compare the performance of classification methods, we use the following performance evaluation measures: precision, recall, accuracy, and F1, which are typical metrics for classification modeling. Features of all four groups are used by the three methods. Table 4.6 shows the modeling results. First, comparing three methods, the C5.0 Decision Tree performs with higher accuracy on the testing set, and Binary Logistic Regression performs similarly to C5.0 on the training set. Next, the C5.0 Decision Tree and Support Vector Machine classify a large number of negative examples correctly. Therefore, the C5.0 Decision Tree significantly outperforms the baseline in terms of recall, accuracy, and F1 metrics.

Table 4.6: Performance comparison of three classification methods.

Data	Training set			Test set		
Method	BLR (baseline)	C5.0	SVM	BLR (baseline)	C5.0	SVM
TP	38	42	37	10	20	16
FP	0	0	0	0	0	0
TN	13	13	13	5	5	5
FN	0	0	1	5	0	1
Precision	1	1	1	1	1	1
Recall	1	1	0.9737	0.6667	1	0.9412
Accuracy	1	1	0.9808	0.75	1	0.9545
F1	1	1	0.9867	0.8000	1	0.9697

C5.0 Model Rule Sets

Based on the analysis of the three modeling methods, the C5.0 Decision Tree outperforms the other two classifiers. We used the model generated by the C5.0 Decision Tree as the basis for further analysis. Moreover, the C5.0 algorithm of IBM SPSS Modeler 18 integrates the Boosting algorithm, which trains the model of information resumption behavior comprehensively and steadily.

The model shown in Figure 4.4 is trained from the C5.0 Decision Tree. There are two rules of logical reasoning structure in information resumption behaviors. Overall, a three-level decision tree is formed, in which the root node contains 55 observations. The number of sessions with/without information resumption behaviors are 42 and 13, respectively, accounting for 76.4% and 23.6%. The tree structure shows that *AveQueryEffectiveRate* is the first best grouping variable. According to the results of the Minimum Description Length Principle (MDLP) entropy grouping, when the *AveQueryEffectiveRate* is less than or equal to 0.5, the *ValidClickRate* is less than or equal to 0.48, and the FamiliarityScores is more than 2, the forecast result is *yes* (with information resumption behaviors). In addition, when the *AveQueryEffectiveRate* is less than or equal to 0.5 and the *AveEditDistance* is greater than 1.6, the forecast is also *yes*.

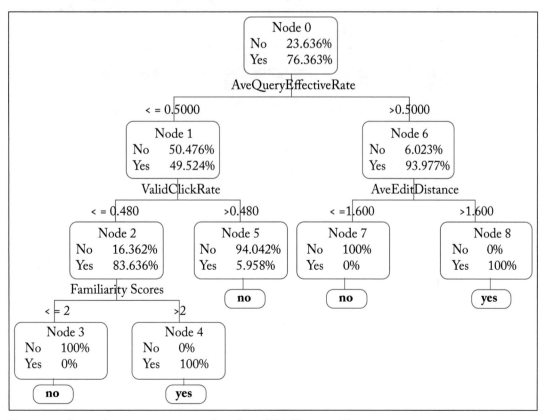

Figure 4.4: Logical reasoning structure based on C5.0 Decision Tree.

Feature Importance Analysis

The importance of features for modeling information resumption behaviors is summarized in Table 4.7 and the calculation is mentioned in Section 4.1.3. Four features are included in the Decision Tree model and have significant effects on information resumption behaviors. Other features do not enter the Decision Tree model and have negligible effects.

As seen in Table 4.7, it appears that the most important feature is users' *familiarity* with a task. Users resume the task after a device transition interruption and acquire more information. Long-term exploration across different devices promotes users' understanding of a task. Features related to the query are also important, including the similarity of queries in information resumption (*AveEditDistance*) and the average rate of valid clicks in the query stream of the information resumption (*AveQueryEffectiveRate*). This indicates that users tend to resume a task by dramatically changing queries. The experience of searching before device transition means that users know more about the task, which allows them to optimize their queries. The optimized queries then help users acquire useful information, which is reflected by the number of effective queries. Furthermore, *ValidClickRate* indicates that users benefit from searching in the pre-transition session. During information resumption, clicks focus on the result areas because the pre-transition searching experience helps users obtain useful results.

Table 4.7: Feature importance for C5.0 Decision Tree model

Feature	Group	Importance
FamiliarityScores	Subjective group	0.33
AveEditDistance	Query group	0.26
AveQueryEffectiveRate	Query group	0.21
ValidClickRate	Click group	0.21

4.3   EXPLORING THE ON-THE-SPOT SEARCH PERFORMANCE IN CROSS-DEVICE SEARCH

Determining the change of search performance in cross-device search is necessary for predicting performance and enhancing the cross-device search system. This section focuses on the on-the-spot search performance in cross-device search.

Cross-device search means that users begin conducting search tasks on a single device, and then resume the tasks on another device (e.g., desktop search→mobile search). In cross-device search, a search session includes one or more queries, and may span multiple devices. Y. Wang et al. (2013) limited the same search session to a single device, and in this section, we also request that the same session occur on a single device. Due to the time limitations, in our experiment, a single cross-device search only includes two sessions: pre-transition and post-transition sessions. Users submitted one or more queries in the pre-transition session, and then they changed the device to resume the tasks in the post-transition session.

In this section, we mainly aim to understand how users' cross-device search performance changes over the search process and whether there are differences in users' search performance between pre-transition and post-transition sessions. Also, we intend to analyze how the search performance changes in regards to different device-transition directions. Furthermore, we also study the search performance when users employ repeated queries to search in the post-transition session.

4.3.1   ON-THE-SPOT SEARCH PERFORMANCE

Effective Search Time

Search time is a common factor to evaluate the user's search performance (Manning and Raghavan, 2010). However, in our study, the search time was same (the duration of search session was 20 min), so the effective search time was used to present the users' temporal performance. In this section, the effective query was defined as the query that could retrieve relevant results. The effective search time was defined as the search time of the effective query. The effective search time of one session was the sum of the search time of all the effective queries in this session.

The proportion of effective search times in the pre-transition session is more than the post-transition session; the difference is significant ($p < 0.01$). This indicates that it is easier for participants to obtain useful information in the pre-transition session; the same is true for desktop-to-mobile transitions ($p < 0.001$). However, the effective search time in the pre-transition session is less than in the post-transition session in mobile-to-desktop transitions, and the difference is not significant (see Table 4.8).

Table 4.8: Average (Standard Deviation) of the Percentage of Valid Click, Effective Search Time, and Satisfaction

	Cross-device (CD)		Desktop-to-mobile (DM)		Mobile-to-desktop (MD)		p-value		
	Pre-switch	Post-switch	Pre-switch	Post-switch	Pre-switch	Post-switch	CD	DM	MD
Search Accuracy	0.844 (0.203)	0.8 (0.252)	0.861 (0.187)	0.743 (0.284)	0.827 (0.22)	0.859 (0.201)	0.261	0.010	0.216
Effective Search Time	0.688 (0.310)	0.591 (0.301)	0.7549 (0.279)	0.522 (0.305)	0.622 (0.329)	0.663 (0.283)	0.008	0.000	0.789
Satisfaction	3.184 (0.901)	3.632 (0.922)	3.203 (0.753)	3.725 (0.849)	3.164 (1.031)	3.537 (0.982)	0.000	0.000	0.006

When was it easier to get useful information for participants in cross-device search process? Figure 4.5 shows the distribution of the proportion of effective queries over time. The darker the color, the more effective the queries, and the easier it is for participants to get useful information. As the figure clearly shows, the proportion of effective queries is lowest at the beginning of the pre-transition and post-transition sessions, which indicates that it is not easy for participants to get useful information quickly at the beginning. However, participants are more likely to obtain useful information after one minute in the pre-transition session than the post-transition session. Over the course of the cross-device search process, the duration of effective searches in the pre-transition session is more than in the post-transition session. In general, the effective pre-transition search time is more than that of the post-transition session, which coincides with Table 4.8, and it is difficult to get useful information in the post-transition session.

Pre-switch	0.16	0.47	0.54		0.59	0.53	0.62	0.55	0.46	0.53	0.49	0.56	0.56	0.50	0.39	0.55	0.49	0.33	0.53	0.53
Post-switch	0.18	0.30	0.48	0.52	0.47	0.50	0.42	0.45	0.56	0.44	0.39	0.52	0.44	0.54	0.50	0.36	0.43	0.32	0.40	0.51
	1	2	3	4	5	6	7	8	9	10	11	12	13	14	15	16	17	18	19	20 (min)

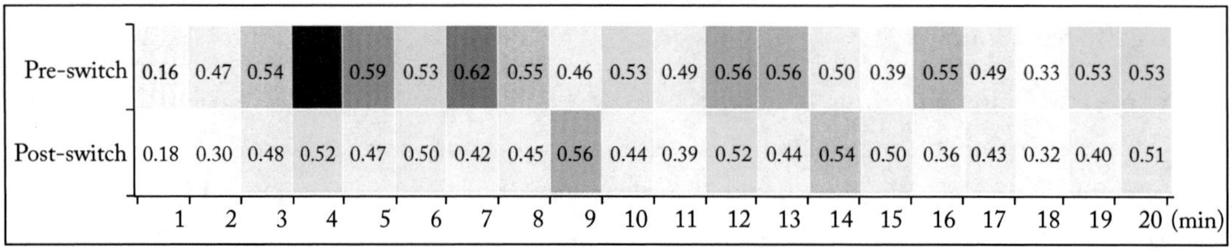

Figure 4.5: The distribution of proportion of effective queries over the time in cross-device search.

Figure 4.6 shows the distribution of proportion of effective queries over time in desktop-to-mobile transitions and mobile-to-desktop transitions. The difference between desktop-to-mobile pre-transition and post-transition sessions coincides with Figure 4.5 and is more distinct. By contrast, the effective pre-transition search time is shorter than that in the post-transition session in mobile-to-desktop transitions, and the duration of effective post-transition search is greater than that in pre-transition session. This indicates that the change of effective search time from pre-transition to post-transition sessions varies with the direction of device transition.

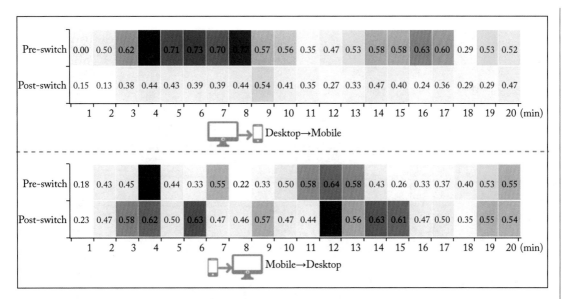

Figure 4.6: The distribution of proportion of effective queries over the time in desktop-to-mobile transitions and mobile-to-desktop transitions.

Percentage of Valid Click

The number of relevant pages found is always used to evaluate task completion rate (Aula and Nordhausen, 2006). In this chapter, the experiment simulated real situations and we did not know which result was relevant in participants' search results. Therefore, participants judged the relevance of each result they clicked. Therefore, the number of relevant pages was not accurate, and the percentage of valid click was used in this section. The percentage of valid clicks is defined as the proportion of relevant results in all the results participants clicked, which can be presented with the following formula:

$$\text{the Percentage of Valid Click} = \frac{\text{the frequency of the relevant results the participants clicked}}{\text{the frequency of all the results participants clicked}}$$

In the Experiment II, 34 participants made judgments on the relevance of 1,921 clicked results. Analyzing the experiment statistics, it was found that compared with the post-transition session, the percentage of valid clicks in the pre-transition session is higher in the cross-device search process. However, there is no significant difference in the percentage of valid clicks between pre-transition and post-transition sessions (see Table 4.8).

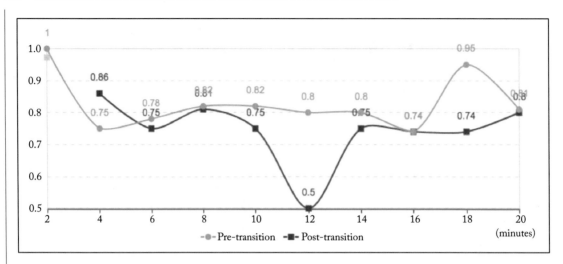

Figure 4.7: The distribution of search accuracy in the search session.

Figure 4.7 presents the distribution of the percentage of valid clicks over time. Most of the time, there is no significant difference of the percentage in valid clicks between pre-transition and post-transition sessions. There is an obvious gap between pre-transition and post-transition sessions in minute 12, which may be caused by individual factors (two participants clicked many irrelevant results in this phase). There is also no score at the initial time of post-transition, because there was no participant clicking the results.

To discuss the change of the percentage of valid clicks based on different device-switching directions, in desktop-to-mobile transitions, the percentage of valid clicks during pre-transition on the desktop is higher than during post-transition on a mobile device, and the difference is significant ($p<0.01$). In mobile-to-desktop transitions, there is no significant difference of the percentage of valid clicks between pre-transition and post-transition sessions. The percentage of valid clicks during the post-transition on the desktop is higher than during pre-transition on a mobile device (see Table 4.8).

The distribution of the percentages of valid clicks in these two device-switching directions is showed in Figure 4.8. When the switching direction is different, the percentage of valid clicks is different. First, the average the percentage of valid clicks of desktop-to-mobile transitions (average percentage of valid click=0.800) is less than that of mobile-to-desktop transitions (average percentage of valid click=0.821). Second, in the search process, the percentage of valid clicks of desktop-to-mobile transitions decreases over time, but the percentage of valid clicks of mobile-to-desktop transitions changes at any time. Third, the gap between the pre-transition and the post-transition sessions in desktop-to-mobile transitions is greater.

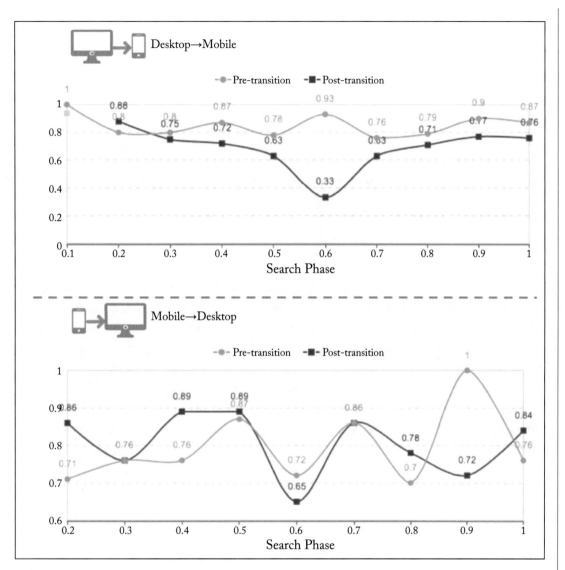

Figure 4.8: The distribution of valid click in desktop-to-mobile transitions and mobile-to-desktop transitions.

nDCG

When users click the results in SERP one by one, nDCG changes. The percentage of valid clicks and effective search time shows the dynamic change of search performance over time, while nDC-G@n shows the dynamic change of search performance over the SERP (search engine results page).

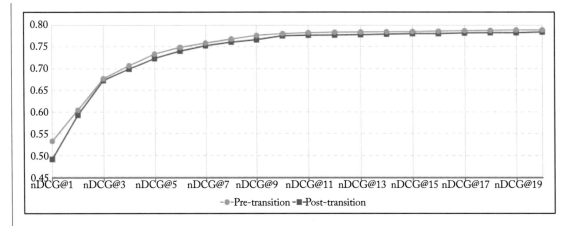

Figure 4.9: The change of nDCG over the cross-device search.

Figure 4.9 presents the change of nDCG over the cross-device search process. As shown, nDCG increases with the rank of the results in SERP that participants clicked. After the 10th result, the nDCG almost stops rising. The nDCG of the pre-transition session is higher than the post-transition session, but the difference between the pre-transition and post-transition sessions is not significant.

Figure 4.10 presents the change of nDCG regarding the different directions of device transition. The nDCG of the post-transition session is higher than the pre-transition session in desktop-to-mobile transitions, and mobile-to-desktop transitions is the opposite. The difference between the pre-transition and post-transition sessions is not significant. As the section above analyzed, users' search performance changed with the direction of device transition. However, unlike the nDCG, for the effective search time and the percentage of valid clicks, the performance of the pre-transition session is better than the post-transition session in desktop-to-mobile transitions, and the performance of mobile-to-desktop transitions is the opposite.

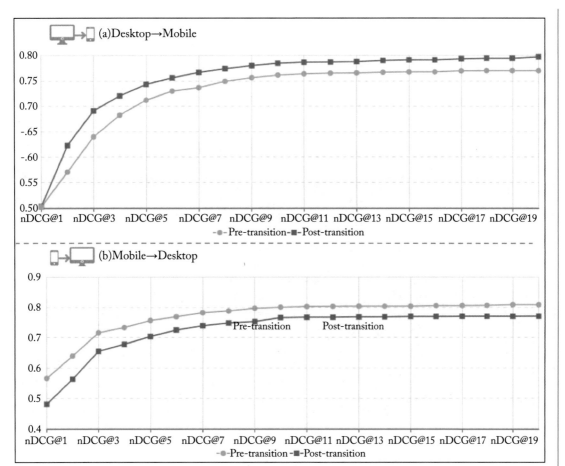

Figure 4.10: The change of nDCG in desktop-to-mobile transitions and mobile-to-desktop transitions

p@n

Participants were asked to judge the relevance of clicked results of the top 20 results. The p@n refers to the precision of the top n results. In this section, p@n was used to present the dynamic change of precision over the whole search process.

Figure 4.11 presents the change of p@n over the cross-device search process. The p@n of the pre-transition session is higher than the post-transition session, but the difference between the pre-transition and post-transition sessions is not significant.

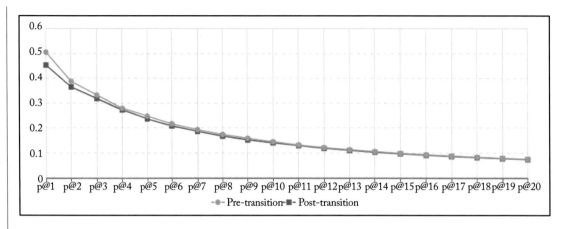

Figure 4.11: The change of p@n over the cross-device search.

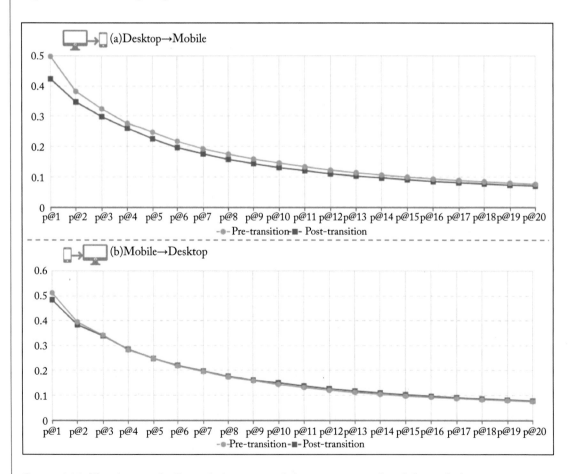

Figure 4.12: The change of p@n in desktop-to-mobile transitions and mobile-to-desktop transitions.

Figure 4.12 presents the change of p@n regarding the different directions of device transition. P@n of the post-transition is higher than the pre-transition session in desktop-to-mobile transitions. However, the difference is not significant. In mobile-to-desktop transitions, the value of the post-transition session is higher than the pre-transition session after p@4. The difference between the pre-transition and post-transition sessions is not significant.

The change of the p@n overall is similar to the change of the effective search time and the percentage of valid clicks. In general, the search performance of the post-transition session is worse than the pre-transition session, but when the direction of transition is mobile-to-desktop, the performance of the post-transition is better than the pre-transition session. The direction of device transition, or the type of device, has an impact on search performance.

Satisfaction

After finishing each session, participants were required to score their satisfaction (5-level Likert scale). Although the search efficiency of the post-transition session was worse than the pre-transition session, the satisfaction score of the post-transition session was higher than the pre-session session, no matter which device-switching direction it was. What we can infer from this conclusion is that participants were satisfied with the current level of search task completion after the post-transition session. Search tasks were continuous and participants obtained what they needed at the end of the search.

From the interview, we found that the post-transition session acted like a supplement to the pre-transition session. When participants obtained what they missed in the pre-session, or when their confidence increased due to familiarity with the topic after the pre-transition search, the satisfaction with the post-transition session easily increased

4.3.2   SEARCH PERFORMANCE OF REPEATED-QUERY AFTER TRANSITION

Re-search behavior is prevalent, and users will commonly utilize repeated queries to search again in the post-transition session (Han et al., 2015a). Teevan et al. (2007) presented the possible classification of re-search based on two dimensions (query string and click-through set). Using repeated queries is just a part of re-search behavior. The way to identify a repeated query differs from language to language. For example, Tyler and Zhang (2012) proposed three types of re-search: same query, minimal change query, and term overlap query. In their study, same-query re-search can only be considered due to the characteristics of the Chinese language. In this section, aside from the same query (meaning the query strings are identical), three types of minimal change query are also considered: extra whitespace, stop words, and non-alphanumerics.

The situation where users enter repeated queries to search in the post-transition session can be explained as follows. Users use qi to search in the pre-transition session, and qj to search in post-transition session. If q_j is the same as q_i (the strings of q_j and q_i are same) or similar to q_i (the main strings of q_j are the same as q_i but q_j has some extra whitespace, stop words, or non-alphanumerics), q_i and q_j are a repeated query pair. In this section, we will compare the search performance of q_i in the pre-transition session and q_j in the post-transition session.

Table 4.9: Search behavior and search performance of re-search in cross-device search

		Cross-device			Desktop-to-Mobile			Mobile-to-Desktop		
		Pre-transition	Post-transition	p-value	Pre-transition	Post-transition	p-value	Pre-transition	Post-transition	p-value
Search Performance	Search accuracy	0.548 (0.450)	0.376 (0.513)	0.007**	0.585 (0.440)	0.342 (0.573)	0.01**	0.515 (0.460)	0.406 (0.458)	0.229
	p@20	0.083 (0.05)	0.078 (0.062)	0.785	0.090 (0.055)	0.064 (0.059)	0.250	0.077 (0.053)	0.090 (0.063)	0.278
Search Behavior	Search time	3.918 (3.298)	2.951 (2.782)	0.004**	4.691 (3.952)	2.842 (2.472)	0.002**	3.243 (2.44)	3.045 (3.042)	0.384
	The number of clicked results	1.670 (1.605)	1.146 (1.061)	0.006**	1.604 (1.250)	1 (0.968)	0.009**	1.727 (1.870)	1.273 (1.130)	0.178
	Clicked results rank	–	-	0.01**	-	-	0.007**	-	-	0.196
	First valid click rank	2.284 (2.315)	2.419 (3.216)	0.504	2.364 (2.275)	2.444 (4.488)	0.915	2.206 (2.384)	2.4 (1.958)	0.321
	Search depth	3.456 (3.463)	2.796 (3.641)	0.120	4.083 (3.847)	2.042 (3.313)	0.004**	2.909 (3.020)	3.455 (3.814)	0.389

Note: *Significant at 0.05 level. ** Significant at 0.01 level. *** Significant at 0.001 level.

In this user study (Experiment II), there were 27 participants (79.41%) repeating a query a total of 103 times in the post-transition session. As Table 4.9 shows, in general, search performance was not as high as in the pre-transition session than when participants used the repeated query to search in the post-transition session. In the post-transition session, the search accuracy and p@20 decreased. A significant difference could be observed in the search accuracy between the pre-transition and post-transition sessions (p<0.01); likewise, desktop-to-mobile transitions were the same. However, in mobile-to-desktop transitions, the p@n of the post-transition session was higher than the pre-transition session. As previously mentioned, the desktop device had a positive effect on p@n.

The changing trend of search performance in repeated-query search processes coincides with the cross-device search process. As Table 4.9 shows, although participants used the repeated query to search again in the post-transition session, the search time was less than that of the pre-transition session.

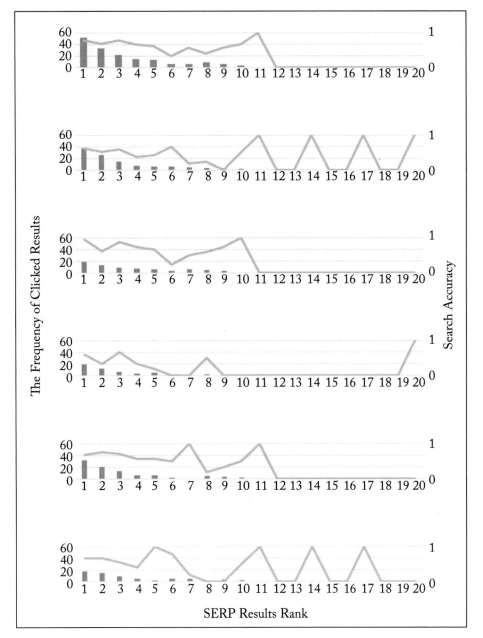

Figure 4.13: The frequency of clicked results and the search accuracy over rank.

Figure 4.13 shows the rank of results participants clicked when they used repeated query to search in the pre-transition and post-transition sessions. In general, during the pre-transition session, participants clicked the top 10 results (the first page of SERP), while some participants clicked relevant results located on the second page of SERP. That means participants were more likely to browse lower-ranking results in the post-transition session. Similar to this finding, the first valid click rank (the rank of the first relevant results that participant clicked) of the post-transition session is lower than that of the pre-transition session. However, it could also be found that the average search depth (the rank of last result that participants clicked (Kelly and Azzopardi, 2015; Wu, Kelly and Avneesh, 2014)) of the post-transition session was lower than that of pre-transition session. That means most participants preferred the top results, even if the second page of SERP was more likely to be clicked in the post-transition session. The frequency of clicked results was more evenly distributed over the results ranked in the pre-transition session.

4.4 PREDICTING SEARCH PERFORMANCE IN CROSS-DEVICE SEARCH

Search performance is one of the essential indicators for search engines. Accurately predicting search performance has been extensively studied in desktop search and mobile search by analyzing information-seeking behavior on SERP (Fox et al., 2005; Huang et al., 2011). Most research predicting search performance is based on single-device behavior features. However, user behaviors are more complicated in cross-device search. Previous work has made great use of MTIs' features to predict search performance in a single-device search, such as action types, touch pressure, and X and Y coordinates of the touch points (Han et al., 2014; Biedert et al., 2012).

Mobile touch interactions (MTI) can also reflect search performance in mobile search, but little is known about how MTIs affect search performance in cross-device search engine result pages. Research on predicting search performance by analyzing MTI in cross-device search is still lacking. In this section, we focus on predicting search performance from MTI on cross-device SERP so that search engines can recommend relevant results to users and achieve better performance. The analysis of this section is also based on Experiment II, which provides the mobile interaction data such as drag up, drag down, drag left, drag right, tap, and press, as well as the time factors in area of SERP on users' mobile phones.

4.4.1 MOBILE TOUCH INTERACTION IN SERP

Based on our dataset, a total of 90,737 MTIs was recorded in our search system. We counted the MTI and their touched areas. The results were shown in Table 4.10.

Table 4.10: Mobile touch interactions and their touched areas			
MTI	Percentage	The Most Frequent Interaction Area (top 6)	Percentage
Drag up	61.54%	Result2 snippet	8.09%
Drag down	22.02%	Result3 snippet	7.05%
Drag right	6.87%	Result4 snippet	4.57%
Drag left	2.96%	Search result: 3	4.47%
Tap	0.81%	Search result: 2	4.44%

From the perspective of MTI, drag up was the most frequent interaction, accounting for 61.54%, followed by drag down. Drag up and drag down interactions are closely related to the small screen of the mobile device. Users need to continue to drag up and drag down in order to access more information. From the perspective of areas, result2 snippet was the most frequent part of the user's interaction, accounting for 8.09%, followed by result3 snippet. To conclude, the most frequent areas users interacted with were ranks two, three, and four.

Table 4.11: The most important areas corresponding to each interaction			
MTI	Area	Frequency	Percentage
Drag up	Result2 snippet	4618	8.27%
Drag down	Result2 snippet	1565	7.83%
Drag right	Result3 snippet	619	9.93%
Drag left	Result2 snippet	278	10.34%
Tap	Result1 title	78	10.66%
Press	Result3 title	2	9.09%

Furthermore, we counted the areas of each MTI (see Table 4.11). From the perspective of each MTI, most drag up, drag down, and drag left interactions took place on the result2 snippet. However, compared to drag left, drag right often interacted with the result3 snippet. Tap, the most frequent MTI, took place at the result1 title, accounting for 10.66%.

In general, a user's first interaction was drag up when interacting with SERP, accounting for 67.65%. This indicates that users tend to drag up to gain more information rather than tap on search results. Most users' first tap decision was the result1 title, followed by the result2 title and result1 snippet (see Table 4.12). According to our dataset, users paid more attention to the first and second results, similar to Hotchkiss et al. (2005).

Table 4.12: First tap decision

First tap decision	Percentage	First tap decision	Percentage
Result1 title	16.86%	Result9 title	1.18%
Result2 title	12.55%	Search result: 2	1.18%
Result1 snippet	10.98%	Result4 snippet	0.78%
Result3 title	6.27%	Result5 snippet	0.78%
Search result: 1	2.75%	Result6 snippet	0.78%
Result2 snippet	2.35%	Search result: 3	0.78%
Result4 title	1.97%	Result2 date	0.39%
Result5 title	1.57%	Result3 snippet	0.39%
Result6 title	1.18%	Result7 title	0.39%
Result7 snippet	1.18%	Search result: 5	0.39%
Result8 title	1.18%	Blank area	34.12%

4.4.2 PREDICTING THE SEARCH PERFORMANCE

Features

A set of 54 features was used to build prediction models. These include features of the MTI types, areas that users interacted with, and inactive time in SERP. Table 4.13 lists the features used in our models; a count of "x5" or "x6" denotes five or six features of that type.

Area group refers to five areas: title, snippet, date, URL, and recording information. For each area, we counted the times, percentage, and maximum of interactions, as well as the result ranking that users most frequently interacted with. Action group includes drag up, drag down, drag right, drag left, tap, and press. For each action, we counted the times, duration, percentage, and so on. This group not only indicates the user's action type but reflects the direction of each action. Inactive time group includes the dwell time in SERP, percentage, and maximum inactive time. A period of inactivity on a touch-enabled mobile device seems to be a good indicator of "reading" behavior (Guo et al., 2013b). In this group, inactive time means the span without any interactions. All these features were counted according to our system logs.

Table 4.13: Features used in prediction models

Group		Feature	Description
Area	Title/snippet/ date/URL/ recording infor- mation	Areacnt (x5)	Times of interact with area
		Areapct (x5)	Percentage of interact with area
		Areamax (x5)	Maximum of interact with area
		Areanum (x5)	Result ranking that users most frequently interacted with
Action	Drag up/drag down/drag right/drag left/ tap/press	Actioncnt (x6)	Times of action
		Actionpct (x6)	Percentage of action
		Actiontime (x6)	Duration of action
		Actiontimepct (x6)	Percentage of duration
		Actionmaxtime (x6)	Maximum duration of single action
Inactive time	/	Dwell time	Dwell time in SERP
		Inactive time	Time without interaction
		Inactivepct	Percentage of inactive time
		Inactivemax	Maximum duration of inactive

Prediction Model

We considered three groups' features for predicting search performance. To better understand which group can attain greater prediction accuracy, we developed four models based on MTIs.

1. **Model A:** This model used the action group features to predict search performance, which has been widely used in previous research (Guo et al., 2013b). This model was regarded as our baseline model.

2. **Model B:** This model was a variant of Model A that adapted the action group features and added the newly proposed area group features. In other words, the features of action and area are used.

3. **Model C:** This model was a variant of Model A that adapted the action group features and added the newly proposed inactive time group features. In other words, the features of action and inactive time are used.

4. **Model D:** This model was a variant of Model A that incorporated all features. In other words, the features of action, area, and inactive time are used.

We treated the search performance prediction as a regression problem, and we applied a simple linear regression model (Han et al., 2015b; Li, X. et al., 2017) to prediction with IBM SPSS Modeler 18.0. We evaluated the search performance by calculating the standard information retrieval measure of NDCG@n (Guo et al., 2011; Järvelin and Kekäläinen, 2000), using the participants' 3-level relevance judgment on the clicked search results from the click questionnaire. We assigned the options of user's relevance feedback in the click questionnaire to the corresponding values; that is, irrelevant was 1, normal relevance was 3, and very relevant was 7. However, users' wrong operations can result in some errors, which affected the results. For example, users forgot to fill the click questionnaire or used other search engines. Finally, a total of 234 questionnaires could be used to build models.

A set of 234 results was used for training and testing. We randomly selected 75% of them to train the model and the remaining 25% were used as the testing set. We varied the cutoff positions (named n) from 1 to 20, increasing by 1 at each step and comparing the prediction accuracy across all n values. The results show that the NDCG@5 performed better than others. Table 4.14 shows the model parameters of predicting NDCG@5.

Table 4.14: Model parameters of predicting NDCG@5		
Model Parameters	R	R-squared
Model A	0.634	0.402
Model B	0.735	0.540
Model C	0.650	0.422
Model D	0.753	0.566

From Table 4.14, we can see that Model D achieves the greatest prediction accuracy, followed by Model B and Model C. This indicates that, compared to the features of inactive time in SERP, area group features are more important in predicting search performance. Moreover, we evaluated the features' importance of each model. Drag up duration is the most important feature in Model A and Model C. However, in Model B and Model D, the maximum duration of single drag up is the most important feature, followed by the percentage of taps. The features related to drag up play a significant role in all models, which indicates that search performance is closely related to the quantity and quality of access information.

Models Compared and Validated

Based on our experiment and features, we chose Model A as the baseline model, which consists of action group features only. We compared and validated the four models by evaluating Root Mean

Square Error (RMSE) (Zhan et al., 2016) using the testing set. RMSE can reflect the precision of models with smaller values, indicating better precision.

Table 4.15: Performance of four models	
Models	**RMSE**
Model A	0.684964
Model B	0.538975
Model C	0.723875
Model D	0.556899

As shown in Table 4.15, all models show significant improvements over the baseline model. Surprisingly, the performance of Model B is the best according to the testing set, with an improved accuracy of 21.31% compared to baseline model. The prediction accuracy of Model D is better than that of Model C, and the accuracy of Model D improves 18.70% compared to baseline model. Our results show that the combination of MTI and touched areas can attain the best performance accuracy. Otherwise, the inactive time in cross-device SERP has no significant difference by comparing Model B with Model C. Constrained by the screen size of mobile devices, users tend to keep sliding to get more information, so inactive time performs worse in predicting mobile search performance.

4.5   SUMMARY

This chapter covers another user study, focusing on users' cross-device search behavior. Interruptions caused by device transition lead to a common phenomenon of repeated searches in cross-device search. In our work, the concept of information preparation is defined by the search behavior on a pre-transition device if the search task is resumed on a post-transition device. We conducted a cross-device search experiment and collected behavior data of information preparation through logs and a questionnaire survey. Four groups of features were extracted and we trained the information preparation behavior model with three machine learning methods. Evaluation results of Binary Logistic Regression, C5.0 Decision Tree, and Support Vector Machine were compared, and finally we selected the model trained by the C5.0 Decision Tree. It showed that dissatisfied click rate, satisfied click rate, first valid click time, valid click rate, and Jaccard distance are included in the model. In order to build a better understanding of the information preparation behavior model, each feature was discussed in depth. This research is novel because studies on repeated search usually focus on behaviors at the resumption stage rather than the preparation stage. Also, although cross-device search has been well studied, repeated search occurring in cross-device search tasks has rarely been explored. We acknowledge that only 34 participants were recruited in the experiment, hence the data seems insufficient.

In addition to considering the complexity of user search behavior, we also studied users' information resumption behavior in cross-device search. First, we defined the information resumption behavior during the subtask in the second search session. Then, we identified features of the search behavior in the latter search session of the device transition, including query group, click group, time group, and context group. We used several machine learning methods to model the behavior using four feature sets, consisting of Binary Logistic Regression (BLR), the C5.0 Decision Tree (C5.0), and Support Vector Machine (SVM). Controlled experimental results using the C5.0 Decision Tree classifier indicate that we can effectively model and analyze information resumption behavior based on cross-device search task. There are information resumption behaviors in cross-device search, and the *FamiliarityScores*, the *AveEditDistance*, the *AveQueryEffectiveRate*, and the *ValidClickRate* are important to the information resumption behavior model. The characteristics of the model are used for predicting the users' task resumption and showing relative information to help people resume previous search memory.

During the analysis of cross-device search behavior, we also presented the on-the-spot change of performance in the cross-device system and analyzed the factors that were most likely to affect search performance. Our results show that users' search performance decreased in the post-transition session. The reason for such phenomena is the users' demand for new information after the pre-transition search. Additionally, we found that search platforms have an impact on the change of search performance. The difference between pre-transition and post-transition sessions in desktop-to-mobile transitions is more distinct than that in mobile-to-desktop transitions. In addition, the change of search performance in repeated-query search process is similar to that in the whole cross-device search process.

Based on the analysis of search performance, we discussed the performance of MTI in cross-device SERP, and our results demonstrate that MTI in cross-device SERP are a high-quality relevance feedback that can predict search performance in cross-device SERP. We divided each search result into five areas and counted the distribution of MTI. Similar to single-device search studies (Granka et al., 2004), ranks one and two were the first tap decision. Furthermore, the second and third results were the most important positions that users interacted with. This is because the second and third results were in the middle of screen. We also found that users began their first tap when they stayed on SERP for about 24 s in the cross-device search, and the first interaction was drag up for most users. In other words, users tended to drag up to get more information when initially accessing SERP. Also, users tended to tap on the result title even though the snippet contains more information, so the snippet sizes should be appropriate for mobile devices (Kim et al., 2017). This can help search engines design a suitable interface and improve information searching. Furthermore, we developed four models to predict search performance; however, unlike previous studies, we only focused on MTI in cross-device SERP. Previous studies found that inactive time has significant positive correlations with document relevance (Han et al., 2015a), but we found that the features of inactive time were not a good indicator of predicting search performance in cross-device SERP. One of the reasons is that the screen sizes of mobile devices increase the chance of interacting with SERP, according to Zhan et al. (2016). Another reason is that users have seen these search results in the pre-transition device and there is no need to read them again.

CHAPTER 5

Discussion and Conclusions

5.1 DISCUSSION

In this book, we conducted two different user experiments to collect user search behavior data. Experiment I was a mobile search experiment conducted in natural settings, and Experiment II was concerned with cross-device search between mobile devices and desktops in a controlled laboratory environment.

5.1.1 CONTEXT FACTORS OF MOBILE SEARCH

Based on Experiment I, we objectively analyzed the relevant data that reflects the participants' mobile search activity. We also analyzed the relevant data in the questionnaires and the structured logs, and combined them with the text content of the interviews to analyze typical participants in order to achieve both quantitative and qualitative analyses.

Our research found that participants searched for information with different languages in the mobile environment. Compared to the phenomenon that ordinary users' information needs were more dispersed, they focused on several particular topics. The number of query and search sessions was higher than in previous research results and reflects the fact that users with higher information literacy will search more frequently. College students could meet their information needs through shorter queries and search sessions since mobile search is more convenient. They also performed more complex search tasks on the mobile phone via multiple strategies. We studied the mobile applications they used and found that they used more APPs in a search session, reflecting diversified search strategies. In addition, mobile search often led to other follow-up activities, such as making a purchase, navigating, sharing search results, and so on.

Based on the users' mobile phone logs, combined with the structured diaries and interviews, about three-fourths of the mobile search sessions were driven by a single motivation, while a quarter were driven by multiple motivations. Different search motivations had the tendency to cross and converge, especially among searches driven by curiosity, time-killing, and learning. What's more, queries in search sessions driven by the former three motivations tended to repeat less frequently than queries about life services, which proves that the former three motivations stimulated more types of information needs, while the life service motivation was stable and uniform. Information needs are driven mainly by three types of motivation: curiosity, learning, and life service. We did not find any significant correlations between emotion changes and motivations. In addition, we found that information search behaviors significantly correlate with multi-dimensional context and motivation. Gender, search activity, importance of the search task, and portal all have significant correlations with information need type, and the information needs driven by different motivations are diverse. Furthermore, the correlations among the dimensional context are significant. Gender, time, place, search activity, relations, importance of the search task, and portal dimensions are all correlated in several ways, and the other dimensions have no significant correlation.

5.1.2 THE RELATIONSHIP BETWEEN MOBILE SEARCH AND APP USAGE

After the above analysis, we examined the relationship between APP usage and mobile search behavior. We found that there are some interactions with other APPs in the mobile search sessions, resulting in the transition between different APPs. These APP interactions are closely related to the mobile searches, such as switching APPs to continue searching, browsing, and sharing the search results. In addition, college students were more inclined to search using specialty APPs and even used more specialty APPs in complex mobile search sessions, while they did not tend to use specialty APPs to search for information about science, news, health, and games. In addition, the type of APPs used in the participants' mobile search could be responsible for the different distribution of search time. College students tended to use a unique APP in a search session, especially compared to the general users. Additionally, the search topic also affected the time duration of the mobile search, especially for health information, which required more time. In addition, when college students used different types of APPs, their search interest and information needs were usually different. It was also found that the differences of search time could be influenced by the type of APPs when searching for the same topics.

Analyzing the relationship between mobile search and APP usage, we found that many APP transitions reflected the users' follow-up actions after searching on mobile phones. We first proposed four patterns of transitions and found that self-transition occurred the most. Before the search, the interactions with communication APPs and the social context could trigger the majority of searches, while there are more actions without queries after searches. Combined with the qualitative study, we believed that the causes of APP-APP transitions are mainly due to the feedback from search results, the interruption while searching, and the follow-up actions after searches. In our work, we found that there were four types of follow-up actions, and participants' information needs for shopping, reference, arts, and computer information could trigger more follow-up actions. Participants might search for different types of information in one search task. The vast majority of follow-up actions occurred within 15 min after the initial query. Also, participants sometimes used several mobile applications or other devices if the needs were complex. We also found that participants often conducted follow-up actions with different apps.

5.1.3 MODELING CROSS-DEVICE SEARCH BETWEEN MOBILE DEVICE AND DESKTOP

The above analysis was mainly concerned with users' search behaviors on a single device, yet it is important to understand users' cross-device search behavior between different devices. Therefore, we conducted another user study (Experiment II) to collect users' cross-device search data. Based on the process of cross-device search, we first analyzed the information preparation behavior. We found that five features—dissatisfied click rate, satisfied click rate, first valid click time, valid click rate, and Jaccard distance—are important when characterizing information preparation behaviors. An in-depth analysis of these features shows that users of information preparation are often dissatisfied with search results, leading to a continuous search on a post-transition device. Further, valid clicks are focused on three periods of the session, meaning effective searches do not occur only at the beginning of information preparation. The average Jaccard distance of queries indicates users preparing a search tended to explore the search by different queries.

In addition, the information preparation behavior does not equal the search behavior on pre-transition devices. Although the information preparation behavior is performed before the device transition, not all pre-transition search behaviors can be regarded as information preparation. We captured 18 features from the search behavior on pre-transition devices, but only 5 features are proven to be of importance to train the information preparation behavior model. On one hand, the information preparation behavior of cross-device search is related to the search behavior of cross-session search. It is shown that queries of information preparation are varied, shown by the wide Jaccard distance. On the other hand, the information preparation behavior of cross-device search is distinguished from the search behavior of cross-session search by feature importance.

When users transitioned to another device to search for information, they might search for the same information for the same task. Considering the complexity of user search behavior, we studied users' information resumption behavior in the cross-device search. First, we defined information resumption behavior, where a user repeats the subtask in the second session. Then we identified features of the search behavior in the latter search session of device transition, including query group, click group, time group, and context group. We used several machine learning methods to model the behavior using four feature sets, consisting of Binary Logistic Regression (BLR), the C5.0 Decision Tree (C5.0), and Support Vector Machine (SVM). Controlled experimental results using the C5.0 Decision Tree classifier for the problem indicate that we can effectively model and analyze the information resumption behavior based on cross-device search tasks. There are information resumption behaviors in cross-device search, and the *FamiliarityScores*, *AveEditDistance*, *AveQueryEffectiveRate*, and *ValidClickRate* are important to the information resumption behavior model. The characteristics of the model are used to predict the users' task resumption and show related information to help people resume the previous search memory.

We also evaluated the users' search performance in cross-device search, finding that users' search performance declined over device transition. In transitions from desktop-to-mobile, the change of users' search performance after switching devices was more distinct than that in mobile-to-desktop transitions. Finally, when users used repeated queries to search after device transitions, the search performance worse than before.

Overall, through our work in this book, we hope that we can give a brief introduction of users' search behavior on mobile phones, and that our work can contribute to help readers understand the cross-device search behavior of users today.

5.2 IMPLICATIONS

5.2.1 BETTER UNDERSTANDING INFORMATION NEEDS BASED ON CONTEXT

Through the analysis of mobile search strategy, we can understand the features of users' search behaviors, and this can enable mobile service providers to better cater to users' search habits and information needs.

Considering context, the system can provide users with more suitable and more specific information. If the user is traveling and searching for neighborhood information, the search system can provide personalized information about traffic or tourist spots according to the location and information need tendency of the user. According to the information need tendency of the user and the task type, ranking the results of Information/Advice or Information/List can meet the needs of the user quickly. TREC conducted research on evaluating the query recommendation based on context and users' interests, both of which have become an essential aspect in research on the personalized mobile search recommendation system. In addition, text, picture, video, and audio search are included as well, which can be the reference for various task designs, such as virtual search system evaluation.

In addition, the research data of mobile search is mainly obtained from logs of a search system on the mobile phone, usually including mobile search information need, search time, and search place. However, the data of this book not only includes logs of a single system, but also logs of the application with search function, which can help contrast research of search behavior on different applications. Mobile search tasks used here are open access to all researchers to support further related studies.

5.2.2 APP RECOMMENDATION IN MOBILE SEARCH

In this book, we found that when college participants searched for information (such as science, news, health, and games), they did not prefer using the corresponding specialty APP. For example, when a participant searched for information about a stock, he/she usually used the browser or social APPs instead of using special financial APPs. This indicates that these professional specialty APPs should improve services to attract users. The findings also can encourage different APPs to open their APIs so users can easily transition between different APPs when searching for information. In addition, some large Internet companies such as Google and Baidu should try to build their APP ecosystem. For example, they could develop or buy different companies in various fields and integrate them into a uniform search portal to provide users with more efficient search services. Once users search for information on one APP, they can easily transition to other APPs to continue their search tasks.

When college students use different types of APPs, the search interests and information needs are also in differentiated distribution. In addition, when they use different types of APPs, the time distribution of the search activity is often different. This feature can be applied to the development of a specialty search engine. For example, the search engine can detect the users' personalized search habits and provide recommended information according to their search times, especially in more demanding time for the searches.

Although our research found that there are many APP transitions in the mobile search process, mobile APPs ideally should not lose any users. Our study on the causes of these transitions indicate that dissatisfaction with content triggered more transitions, which could work for APP recommendation. Multimedia APPs in particular should improve their services, such as by buying more copyrights to provide more multimedia content so as to prevent their users from transferring to other APPs. On the other hand, users are accustomed to employing different APPs at the same time and there are some correlations between different types of APPs in the process of mobile search. Therefore, it is necessary to set up collaborations between related APPs to increase the number of users. For instance, mobile search engines could offer search recommendations from related APPs to help users immediately transfer to various APPs. As for instant communication APPs, it's necessary for them to provide convenient services for searching, because there are many transitions to browser and search engine APPs from instant communication APPs.

5.2.3   PREDICTION IN CROSS-DEVICE SEARCH

Through the study of cross-device search behavior, the concept of information preparation and the method of modeling information preparation behavior can provide personalized support to cross-device search. Cross-device users with information preparation behaviors are likely to repeat a search on the post-transition device. Therefore, detecting information preparation behavior is useful to target potential cross-device search users in advance. As shown in the feature analysis, features related to clicking are important to the information preparation behavior. It is suggested that search engines providing cross-device supporting services should attach importance to users' clicking data.

Due to the wide Jaccard distance of queries during information preparation, related queries recommended that support of cross-device search should be different from queries issued previously.

As people have information resumption behaviors in Session 2 (post-transition search session), the findings of our model suggest that a person's history may be useful, especially people's interaction comparison of the pre-transition session and the post-transition session in cross-device search. When capturing users' unique query features, the search system can better provide the related viewed information and help people recall previous search memory. Query and click should be combined to support and predict the people's resumption of interrupted tasks.

The model in Section 4.2 shows that the *AveQueryEffectiveRate* and the *ValidClickRate* are conducive to resumption of information when they are lower (*AveQueryEffectiveRate* <=0.5, *ValidClickRate* <=0.48). This can help to understand the efficiency of query; that is, when users click fewer search results, a common previous query would be recommended by search engine. Search engines properly use the user's search history and synchronize search records between different devices. If resumption is predicted when they are on the search engine homepage, the search box could populate their pre-transition query. At the same time, it is essential to shift that improvement of a single query's result relevance to help people perform complex, multi-session tasks for modern search engines.

Meanwhile, search performance and search behavior differ greatly when the device-transition direction is different. Therefore, the device-transition direction should be considered when the search system offers assistance to users, e.g., when a person searches something on the mobile device first and then he/she wants to transition to the desktop to continue the search tasks. It is very possible that search performance in the post-transition session is at least as good as before transitioning, if not better. Therefore, cross-device search systems do not need to provide extra aid in case the aid affects users' search strategy. Our study about on-the-spot search performance explored the dynamic change of users' search performance in the cross-device search process and analyzed the factors that affected the search performance. These conclusions provide a reference for future performance-predicting works. Those factors mentioned above can be used to predict the change of search performance, especially the post-transition search performance, which will be our future research direction.

5.3 LIMITATIONS

Of course, there are some limitations to this book. As the study is focused on college students and the user volume is small, the resulting conclusions cannot be extrapolated to cover all user groups, and therefore lack universality. In addition, because of the limitations of the AWARE software and the requirement of user privacy protection, we cannot analyze the causes of APP-APP transition triggered by external factors. Therefore, there may be more types of follow-up actions that we did not recognize.

As for research about cross-device search behavior, our dataset was based on user experiment rather than real cross-device search data and we mainly analyzed the device transitions between two different devices.

5.4   CONCLUSIONS

In this book, we gave a systematic review of the current mobile search research and studied users' mobile search behavior from different perspectives. We analyzed users' mobile search strategies and offered context-based mobile search task collection, which can be used to evaluate mobile search engines. In addition, we combined the mobile search with APP usage to give a more in-depth analysis. We also focused on users' cross-device search behavior. We modeled the information preparation behavior and information resumption behavior in cross-device searches, and evaluated the search performance in cross-device search.

In the future, we will build the model of users' follow-up actions caused by complex search needs or tasks. In addition, we will continue to explore more characteristics of transition between APPs in mobile search, such as the time gap of transition, and summarize the behavior model to better support the transitions of APPs in mobile search. Future work will also concentrate on the influence of social factors on transitions and the prediction of transitions.

Furthermore, we will continue to study cross-device search behavior and focus on extending the sample size. We will integrate both preparation and resumption behaviors to frame behaviors of a complete cross-device search; we also will focus on performance prediction and the machine learning methods that will be used to predict search performance. In addition, we will extend this research and take the types of search tasks and different screen sizes of devices into consideration.

References

Agichtein, E., White, R.W., Dumais, S.T., and Bennet, P.N. (2012). Search, interrupted: understanding and predicting search task continuation. In *Proceedings of the 35th International ACM SIGIR Conference on Research and Development in Information Retrieval*, ACM, New York, 315–324. DOI: 10.1145/2348283.2348328. 14, 106, 113

Agrawal R., Yu X., King I., and Zajac R. (2011). Enrichment and reductionism: Two approaches for web query classification. In: Lu BL., Zhang L., Kwok J. (eds) *Neural Information Processing. ICONIP 2011. Lecture Notes in Computer Science*, Springer, Berlin, Heidelberg. 4

Ahn, J.W., Brusilovsky, P., He, D.Q., Grady, J., and Li, Q. (2008). Personalized web exploration with task models. In *Proceedings of the 17th International Conference on World Wide Web*, ACM, New York, 1–10. DOI: 10.1145/1367497.1367499. 17

Amin, A., Townsend, S., Ossenbruggen, J. V., and Hardman, L. (2009). Fancy a drink in canary wharf?: a user study on location-based mobile search. Ifip Tc 13 International Conference on Human-Computer Interaction, (5726), 736-749. 47

App Annie. (2016). App Annie 2015 retrospective. http://go.appannie.com/report-app-annie-retrospective-2015-methodology (accessed October 12, 2017). 1

Arzenšek, B. and Heričko, M. (2014). Criteria for selecting mobile application testing tools. In *CEUR Workshop Proceedings*. 1-8. 4

Aula, A., Jhaveri, N., and Käki, M. (2005). Information search and re-access strategies of experienced Web users. In *Proceedings of the 14th international conference on World Wide Web (WWW '05)*. ACM, Chiba, Japan, 583-592. DOI:10.1145/1060745.1060831. 14

Aula A. and Nordhausen K. (2006). Modeling successful performance in Web searching. *Journal of the American Society for Information Science and Technology*, 57(2), 1678-1693. DOI: 10.1002/asi.20340. 119

Baeza-Yates, R., Dupret, G., and Velasco, J. (2007). A study of mobile search queries in Japan. In *Proceedings of the International World Wide Web Conference*, Banff, Canada. 4

Baron, J.R., Lewis, D.D., and Oard, D.W. (2006). TREC 2006 legal track overview. I*n Proceedings of the Fifteenth Text Retrieval Conference (TREC 2006)*. 1–2. 7, 66

Biedert, R., Dengel, A., Buscher, G., and Vartan, A. (2012). Reading and estimating gaze on smart phones. In *Proceedings of the Symposium on Eye Tracking Research and Applications*, ACM, New York, 385–388. DOI: 10.1145/2168556.2168643. 128

Böhmer, M., Hecht, B., Schöning, J., Krüger, A., and Bauer, G. (2011). Falling asleep with Angry Birds, Facebook and Kindle: A large scale study on mobile application usage. In *Proceedings of theInternational Conference on Human Computer Interaction with Mobile Devices and Services*. ACM, New York, 47–56. DOI: 10.1145/2037373.2037383. 11, 12, 13, 80, 89

Broder, A. (2002). A taxonomy of web search. *ACM SIGIR Forum*, 36(2), 3-10. DOI: 10.1145/792550.792552. 47

Cao, H., Wolfson, O., Xu, B., and Yin, H. (2005). MOB-DIC: mobile discovery of local resources in peer-to-peer wireless network. *IEEE Data Eng Bull*, 28, 11-18. 3

Carpineto, C., Mizzaro, S., Romano, G., and Snidero, M. (2009). Mobile information retrieval with search results clustering: Prototypes and evaluations. *Journal of the American Society for Information Science and Technology*, 60(5), 877–895. DOI: 10.1002/asi.v60:5. 7

Carrascal, J.P. and Church, K. (2015). An in-situ study of mobile app and mobile search interactions. In *Proceedings of the Annual ACM Conference on Human Factors in Computing Systems*. ACM, New York, 2739–2748. DOI: 10.1145/2702123.2702486. 12, 13, 79, 80, 95

Carterette, B., Pavlu, V., Kanoulas, E., Aslam, J.A., and Allan, J. (2008). Evaluation over thousands of queries. In *Proceedings of the 31st Annual International ACM SIGIR Conference on Research and Development in Information Retrieval*. ACM, New York, 2008: 651–658. DOI: 10.1145/1390334.1390445. 8

Church, K. and Oliver, N. (2011). Understanding mobile web and mobile search use in today's dynamic mobile landscape. In *Proceedings of the Mobile HCI 2011. Stockholm, Sweden: Swedish Institute of Computer Science*, 67–76. DOI:10.1145/2037373.2037385. 4, 5

Church, K., Smyth, B., Bradley, K., and Cotter, P. (2008). A large scale study of European mobile search behavior. In *Proceedings of the International Conference on Human Computer Interaction with Mobile Devices and Services*. ACM, New York, 13–22. DOI: 10.1145/1409240.1409243. 6, 7, 40, 41, 42, 43, 83, 98

Church, K. and Smyth, B. (2008a). Understanding mobile information needs. In *Proceedings of the International Conference on Human Computer Interaction with Mobile Devices and Services*. ACM, New York, 493–494. DOI: 10.1145/1409240.1409325. 41

Church, K., and Smyth, B. (2008b). Who, what, where and when: a new approach to mobile search. *Proceedings of the 13th International Conference on Intelligent User Interfaces*, pp. 309-312. ACM. DOI: 10.1145/1378773.1378817. 5

Church, K., Smyth, B., Cotter, P., and Bradley K. (2007). Mobile information access: A study of emerging search behavior on the mobile Internet. *ACM Transactions on the Web (TWEB)*, 1(1), 1–38. DOI: 10.1145/1232722.1232726. 4, 6, 41, 42, 45

Claypool, M., Le, P., Wased, M., and Brown, D. (2001). Implicit interest indicators. *In Proceedings of the 6th International Conference on Intelligent User Interfaces*, ACM, New York, 33–40. DOI: 10.1145/359784.359836. 17

Cleverdon, C. (1967). The Cranfield tests on index language devices. *Aslib Proceedings*, 19(6), 173–194. DOI: 10.1108/eb050097. 7, 8

Cui, J., Wen, F., and Tang, X. (2008). Real time Google and live image search re-ranking. In *Proceedings of the 16th ACM International Conference on Multimedia*. ACM, New York, 729–732. DOI: 10.1145/1459359.1459471. 16, 47

Czerwinski, M., Horvitz, E., and Wilhite, S. (2004). A diary study of task switching and interruptions. In *Proceedings of the SIGCHI Conference on Human Factors in Computing Systems (CHI'04)*. ACM, Vienna, Austria,175–182. DOI:10.1145/985692.985715. 15

Daoud, M., Lechani, L.T., and Boughanem, M. (2009). Towards a graph-based user profile modeling for a session-based personalized search. *Knowledge and Information Systems*, 21(3), 365–398. DOI: 10.1007/s10115-009-0232-0. 7, 79

Dearman, D. and Pierce, J.S. (2008). It's on my other computer!: computing with multiple devices. In *Proceedings of the IGCHI Conference on Human Factors in Computing Systems*. ACM, New York, 767–776. DOI: 10.1145/1357054.1357177.

Eickhoff, C., Teevan, J., White, R., and Dumais, S. (2014). Lessons from the journey: a query log analysis of within-session learning. In *Proceedings of the 7th ACM International Conference on Web Search and Data Mining*. ACM, New York, 223–232. DOI: 10.1145/2556195.2556217. 6, 32, 47

Ekstrand-Abueg, M., Pavlu, V., Kato, M., Sakai, T., Yamamoto, T., and Iwata, M. (2013). Exploring semi-automatic nugget extraction for Japanese one click access evaluation. In *Proceedings of the 36th International ACM SIGIR Conference on Research and Development in Information Retrieval*. ACM, New York, 749–752. DOI: 10.1145/2484028.2484153. 7

Esmaili, K.S., Abolhassani, H., Neshati, M., Behrangi, E., Rostami, A., and Nasiri, M.M. (2007). Mahak: A test collection for evaluation of farsi information retrieval systems. In *Proceedings of the IEEE/ACS International Conference on Computer Systems and Applications*. IEEE, New York, 639–644. DOI: 10.1109/AICCSA.2007.370697. 8

Falaki, H., Mahajan, R., Kandula, S., Lymberopoulos, D., Govindan, R., and Estrin, D. (2010). Diversity in smartphone usage. In *Proceedings of the International Conference on Mobile Systems*,

Applications, and Services. ACM, New York, 179–194. DOI: 10.1145/1814433.1814453. 11, 12, 81, 89

Ferreira, D., Goncalves, J., Kostakos, V., Barkhuus, L., and Dey, A.K. (2014). Contextual experience sampling of mobile application micro-usage. In *Proceedings of the International Conference on Human Computer Interaction with Mobile Devices and Services.* ACM, New York, 91–100. DOI: 10.1145/2628363.2628367. 11

Fox, S., Karnawat, K., Mydland, M., Dumais, S., and White, T. (2005). Evaluating implicit measures to improve web search. *ACM Transactions on Information Systems*, 23(2), 147–168. DOI: 10.1145/1059981.1059982. 17, 113, 128

Fu, B., Lin, J., Li, L., Faloutsos, C., Hong, J., and Sadeh, N. (2013). Why people hate your app: making sense of user feedback in a mobile app store. In *Proceedings of the ACM SIGKDD International Conference on Knowledge Discovery and Data Mining.* ACM, New York, 1276–1284. DOI: 10.1145/2487575.2488202. 12

Gan, C.L. and Balakrishnan, V. (2016). Enhancing classroom interaction via IMMAP-an interactive mobile messaging App. *Telematics and Informatics*, 34(1), 230–243. DOI: 10.1016/j. tele.2016.05.007. 12

Gasimov, A., Magagna, F., and Sutanto, J. (2010). CAMB: Context-aware mobile browser. In *Proceedings of the 9th International Conference on Mobile and Ubiquitous Multimedia*, Limassol, Cyprus: Cyprus University of Technology and Frederick University, 22. DOI: 10.1145/1899475.1899497. 5

Google and Nielsen. (2013). Mobile Search Moments: Understanding how mobile drives conversions. http://think.withGoogle.com/databoard/media/pdfs/creating-moments-that-matter_research-studies.pdf (accessed October 13, 2017). 13, 95, 99

Google, IpsosMediaCT and Purchased, (2014). Understanding consumer's local search behavior. http://think.storage.googleapis.com/docs/how- (accessed August 9, 2017). 1, 13

Gouin-Vallerand, C. and Mezghani, N. (2014). An analysis of the transitions between mobile application usages based on Markov chains. In *Proceedings of the International Joint Conference on Pervasive and Ubiquitous Computing*, 373–378. DOI: 10.1145/2638728.2641700. 13

Granka, L.A., Joachims, T., and Gay, G. (2004). Eye-tracking analysis of user behavior in WWW search. In *Proceedings of the 27th Annual International ACM SIGIR Conference on Research and Development in Information Retrieval*, ACM, New York, 478–479. DOI: 10.1145/1008992.1009079. 134

Gui, F., Adjouadi, M., and Rishe, N. (2009). A contextualized and personalized approach for mobile search. In *Proceedings of the 2009 International Conference on Advanced Information*

Networking and Applications Workshops, IEEE Computer Society, Washington, DC, USA, 966-971. 3

Guo, Q. and Agichtein, E. (2010). Ready to buy or just browsing?: detecting web searcher goals from interaction data. In *Proceedings of the 33rd International ACM SIGIR Conference on Research and Development in Information Retrieval*, ACM, New York, 130–137. DOI: 10.1145/1835449.1835473. 106, 113

Guo, Q., Jin, H.J., Lagun, D., Yuan, S., and Agichtein, E. (2013a). Towards estimating web search result relevance from touch interactions on mobile devices. In *Proceedings of the CHI '13 Extended Abstracts on Human Factors in Computing Systems*. ACM, New York, 1821–1826. DOI: 10.1145/2468356.2468683. 17

Guo, Q., Jin, H.J., Lagun, D., Yuan, S., and Agichtein, E. (2013b). Mining touch interaction data on mobile devices to predict web search result relevance. In *Proceedings of the 36th International ACM SIGIR Conference on Research and Development in Information Retrieval*, ACM, New York, 153–162. DOI: 10.1145/2484028.2484100. 130, 131

Guo, Q., Yuan, S., and Agichtein, E. (2011). Detecting success in mobile search from interaction. In *Proceedings of the 34th International ACM SIGIR Conference on Research and Development in Information Retrieval*, ACM, New York, 1220–1230. DOI: 10.1145/2009916.2010133. 132

Hagen, M., Gomoll, J., Beyer, A., and Stein, B. (2013). From search session detection to search mission detection, In *Proceedings of the 10th Conference on Open Research Areas in Information Retrieval*, ACM, New York, 85–92. 7

Han, S., Zhen, Y., and He, D. (2015a). Understanding and supporting cross-device web search for exploratory tasks with mobile touch interactions. *ACM Transactions on Information Systems (TOIS)*, 33(4), 1–34. DOI: 10.1145/2738036. 5, 14, 15, 16, 17, 23, 79, 112, 125, 134

Han, S., He, D., Yue, Z., and Brusilovsky, P. (2015b). Supporting cross-device web search with social navigation-based mobile touch interactions. In *Proceedings of the International Conference on User Modeling, Adaptation, and Personalization*, Springer, Germany, 143–155. DOI: 10.1007/978-3-319-20267-9_12 1.2.1 1.4.2. 5, 15, 16, 132

Han, S., He, D., and Chi, Y. (2017). Understanding and modeling behavior patterns in cross-device web search. *Proceedings of the Association for Information Science and Technology*, 54(1), 150-158. DOI: 10.1002/pra2.2017.14505401017. 5, 15

Han, S., Hsiao, J., and Parra, D. (2014). A study of mobile information exploration with multi-touch interactions. In *Proceedings of the International Conference on Social Computing, Behavior-*

al-Cultural Modeling, and Prediction. ACM, New York, 269–276. DOI: 10.1007/978-3-319-05579-4_33. 128

Hassan, A., White, R.W., Dumais, S.T., and Yimin, W. (2014). Struggling or exploring?: disambiguating long search sessions. In *Proceedings of the 7th ACM International Conference on Web Search and Data Mining.* ACM, New York, 53–62. DOI: 10.1145/2556195.2556221. 7, 47

He, D., Göker, A., and Harper, D.J. (2002). Combining evidence for automatic Web session identification. *Information Processing and Management*, 38(5), 727–742. DOI: 10.1016/s0306-4573(01)00060-7. 32, 45

Hinze, A. M., Chang, C., and Nichols, D. M. (2010). Contextual queries express mobile information needs. In *Proceedings of the International Conference on Human Computer Interaction with Mobile Devices and Services.* ACM, New York, 327–336. DOI: 10.1145/1851600.1851658. 33, 47

Hou, Z., Wang, C., Ma, Y., et al. (2016). A study of design research of APP guidance based on user search behavior. http://www.paper.edu.cn/releasepaper/content/201601-282 (accessed April 10, 2017). 13

Hotchkiss, G., Alston, S., and Edwards, G. (2005). Eye tracking study. Research white paper, Enquiro Search Solutions Inc. 129

Huang, J., White, W., and Dumais, S. (2011). No clicks, no problem: using cursor movements to understand and improve search. In *Proceedings of the SIGCHI Conference on Human Factors in Computing Systems.* ACM, New York, 1225–1234. DOI: 10.1145/1978942.1979125.128

IiMedia Research Group. (2017). 2017H1 China mobile search market research report. http://www.iimedia.cn/53193.html (accessed September 3, 2017). 1, 51

Jansen, B.J., Spink, A., and Kathuria, V. (2006). How to define searching sessions on web search engines. In *Proceedings of the 8th Knowledge Discovery on the Web International Conference on Advances in Web Mining and Web Usage Analysis.* Springer-Verlag, New York, 92–109. DOI: 10.1007/978-3-540-77485-3_6. 4, 42, 43, 45, 49

Jansen, B.J., Campbell, G., and Gregg, M. (2010). Real time search user behavior. In *Proceedings of the CHI '10 Extended Abstracts on Human Factors in Computing Systems.* ACM, New York, 3961–3966. DOI: 10.1145/1753846.1754086. 16

Jansen, B.J., Liu, Z., Weaver, C., Campbell, G., and Gregg, M. (2011). Real time search on the web: queries, topics, and economic value. *Information Processing and Management*, 47(4), 491–506. DOI: 10.1016/j.ipm.2011.01.007. 6, 16

Järvelin, K. and Kekäläinen, J. (2000). IR evaluation methods for retrieving highly relevant documents. In *Proceedings of the 23rd Annual International ACM SIGIR Conference on Research and Development in Information Retrieval*, ACM, New York, 41–48. DOI: 10.1145/345508.345545. 132

Jesdabodi, C. and Maalej, W. (2015). Understanding usage states on mobile devices. *In Proceedings of the International Joint Conference on Pervasive and Ubiquitous Computing*. ACM, New York, 1221–1225. DOI: 10.1145/2750858.2805837. 11, 12

Jiang, J., He, D.Q., Kelly, D., and James, A. (2017). Understanding ephemeral state of relevance. In *Proceedings of the 2017 Conference on Conference Human Information Interaction and Retrieval*. ACM, New York, 137–146. DOI: 10.1145/3020165.3020176.

Joachims, T., Granka, L., Pan, B., Hembrooke, H., Radlinski, F., and Gay, G. (2007). Evaluating the accuracy of implicit feedback from clicks and query reformulations in Web search. *ACM Transactions on Information Systems*, 25(2), 1–27. DOI: 10.1145/1229179.1229181. 17

Jones, K.S. (1976). Information retrieval test collections. *Journal of Documentation*, 32(1), 59–75. DOI: 10.1108/eb026616. 8

Kahveci, B., Altıngövde, İ.S., and Ulusoy, Ö. (2016). Integrating social features into mobile local search. *Journal of Systems and Software*, 122(12), 155–164. DOI: 10.1016/j.jss.2016.09.013. 12

Kamvar, M. and Baluja, S. (2006). A large scale study of wireless search behavior: Google mobile search. In *Proceedings of the SIGCHI Conference on Human Factors in Computing Systems*. ACM, New York, 701–709. DOI: 10.1145/1124772.1124877. 5, 6

Karlson, A.K., Iqbal, S., Meyers, B., Ramos, G., Lee, K., and Tang, J. (2010). Mobile taskflow in context: a screenshot study of smartphone usage. In *Proceedings of the SIGCHI Conference on Human Factors in Computing Systems* (CHI '10). ACM, Atlanta, Georgia, 2009-2018. DOI:10.1145/1753326.1753631. 14

Kato, M.P., Ekstrand-Abueg, M., Pavlu, V., Sakai, T., Yamamoto, T., and Iwata, M. (2013). Overview of the NTCIR-10 1CLICK-2 Task[C]. /NTCIR. 2013. 11

Kelly, D. and Azzopardi L. (2015). How many results per page? A Study of SERP Size, search behavior and user experience. In *Proceedings of the 38th International ACM SIGIR Conference on Research and Development in Information Retrieval*. ACM, New York, 183–192. DOI: 10.1145/2766462.2767732. 128

Khalid, H., Shihab, E., Nagappan, M., and Hassan, A.E. (2015). What do mobile App users complain about? *IEEE Software*, 32(3), 70–77. DOI: 10.1109/ms.2014.50. 12

Kim, Y.H., Hassan, A., White, R.W., and Wang, Y.M. (2013). Playing by the rules: mining query associations to predict search performance. In *Proceedings of the 6th ACM International Conference on Web Search and Data Mining*, ACM, New York, 133–142. DOI: 10.1145/2433396.2433414. 17

Kim, H. K. (2013). Architecture for adaptive mobile applications. *International Journal of Bio-Science and Bio-Technology*, 5(5), 197-210. 4

Kim, J.W., Thomas, P., Sankaranarayana, R., Gedeon, T., and Yoon, H.J. (2017). What snippet size is needed in mobile web search?. In *Proceedings of the 2017 Conference on Conference Human Information Interaction and Retrieval*, ACM, New York, 97–106. DOI: 10.1145/3020165.3020173. 134

Kiseleva, J. (2015). Using contextual information to understand searching and browsing behavior. In *Proceedings of the SIGIR'15 Santiago, 38th Special Interest Group on Information Retrieval Conference*. Santiago, Chile: Association for Computing Machinery, 1059. DOI:10.1145/2766462.2767852. 5

Komaki, D., Hara, T., and Nishio, S. (2012). How does mobile context affect people's web search behavior?: A diary study of mobile information needs and search behaviors. In *Proceedings of the International Conference on Advanced Information Networking and Applications*. AINA. DOI: 10.1109/AINA.2012.134. 33

Kong, W.Z., Li, R., Jie, L., Zhang, A., Chang, Y., and Allan, J. (2015). Predicting search intent based on pre-search context. In *Proceedings of the SIGIR'15 Santiago, 38th Special Interest Group on Information Retrieval Conference*. Santiago, Chile: ACM, 503–512. DOI:10.1145/2766462.2767757. 5

Kotov, A., Bennett, P.N., White, R.W., Dumais, S.T., and Teevan, J. (2011). Modeling and analysis of cross-session search tasks. In *Proceedings of the 34th International ACM SIGIR Conference on Research and Development in Information Retrieval*, ACM, New York, 5–14. DOI: 10. 1145/2009916.2009922. 7, 14, 17, 106, 113, 114

Li, X., Liu, Y., Cai, R., and Ma, S.P. (2017). Investigation of user search behavior while facing heterogeneous search services. In *Proceedings of the 10th ACM International Conference on Web Search and Data Mining*, ACM, New York, 161–170. DOI: 10.1145/3018661.3018673. 132

Li, Y., Xu, P., Langun, D., and Navalpakkam, V. (2017). Towards measuring and inferring user interest from gaze. In *Proceedings of the 26th International Conference on World Wide Web Companion*, ACM, New York, 525–533. DOI: 10.1145/3041021.3054182. 17

Li, J., Huffman, S., and Tokuda. (2009). A good abandonment in mobile and PC internet search. In *Proceedings of the International ACM SIGIR Conference on Research and Development in Information Retrieval*. ACM, New York, 43–50. DOI: 10.1145/1571941.1571951. 8

Li, J. and Yan, H. (2008). Chinese web retrieval test collections: construction, analysis and application. *Journal of Chinese Information Processing*, 22(1), 877–895. DOI: 10.3969/j.issn.1003-0077.2008.01.005. 7

Liu, X. and Wu, W. (2015). Learning context-aware latent representations for context-aware collaborative filtering. In *Proceedings of the SIGIR'15 Santiago, 38th Special Interest Group on Information Retrieval Conference*. Santiago, Chile: Association for Computing Machinery, 887–890. DOI:10.1145/2766462.2767775. 5

Liu, P. and Li, Z. (2012). Task complexity: A review and conceptualization framework. *International Journal of Industrial Ergonomics*, 42(6), 553-568. DOI: 10.1016/j.ergon.2012.09.001. 23

Manning, C.D. and Raghavan, P. (2010). *Introduction to Information Retrieval*. Posts and Telecom Press. 8 , 117

Menemenis, F., Papadopoulos, S., Bratu, B., Waddington, S., and Kompatsiaris, Y. (2008). AQUAM: automatic query formulation architecture for mobile applications. In *Proceedings of the 7th International Conference on Mobile and Ubiquitous Multimedia*. ACM, New York, 32–39. DOI: 10.1145/1543137.1543144. 6

Miller, F. P., Vandome, A. F., Mcbrewster, J., (2010). Mobile local search. Alphascript Publishing. Access at: https://www.morebooks.de/store/pt/book/mobile-local-search/isbn/978-613-4-06669-3. 3

Montañez G.D., White R.W., and Huang, X. (2014). Cross-device search. In *Proceedings of the 23rd ACM International Conference on Conference on Information and Knowledge Management*. ACM, New York, 1669–1678. DOI: 10.1145/2661829.2661910. 5, 14, 15, 16 , 17, 84

Mollá, D., Martinez, D., and Amini, I. (2013). Towards information retrieval evaluation with reduced and only positive judgments. In *Proceedings of the 18th Australasian Document Computing Symposium*. ACM, New York, 109–112. DOI: 10.1145/2537734.2537748. 8

Neustar. (2014). Cross Device Local Search: A Guide for Businesses: http://www.neustarlocaleze.biz/docs/neustar-comscore-whitepaper-final.pdf (accessed July 9, 2017). 13, 98

Park, E. and Ohm, J. (2014). Factors influencing users' employment of mobile map services. Telematics and Informatics, 31(2): 253. DOI: 10.1016/j.tele.2013.07.002 (accessed September 10, 2017). 5

Pavani M. and Teja G.R. (2015). Online clustering algorithm for restructuring user web search results. In: Satapathy S., Biswal B., Udgata S., Mandal J. (eds) *Proceedings of the 3rd Inter-*

national Conference on Frontiers of Intelligent Computing: Theory and Applications (FICTA) 2014. Springer, Cham. DOI: 10.1007/978-3-319-11933-5_4. 4

Piwowarski, B. and Zaragoza, H. (2007). Predictive user click models based on click-through history. In *Proceedings of the Sixteenth ACM Conference on Conference on Information and Knowledge Management.* ACM, New York, 175–182. DOI: 10.1145/1321440.1321467. 6

Raman, K., Bennett, P.N., and Collins-Thompson, K. (2013). Toward whole-session relevance: exploring intrinsic diversity in web search. In *Proceedings of the 36th International ACM SIGIR Conference on Research and Development in Information Retrieval.* ACM, New York, 463–472. DOI: 10.1145/2484028.2484089. 7

Ravana, S.D., Rajagopal, P., and Balakrishnan, V. (2015). Ranking retrieval systems using pseudo relevance judgments[J]. *Aslib Journal of Information Management,* 67(6): 700–714. DOI: 10.1108/AJIM-03-2015-0046. 8

Rodgers, U. (1999). *Oracle: A Database Developer's Guide.* Prentice Hall PTR, Upper Saddle River, NJ, USA. 4

Rose, D.E. and Levinson, D. (2004). Understanding user goals in Web search. In *Proceedings of the 13th International Conference on World Wide Web.* 13–19. DOI: 10.1145/988672.988675. 67

Sakai, T., Kato, M.P., and Song, Y.I. (2011). Click the search button and be happy: evaluating direct and immediate information access. In *Proceedings of the 20th ACM International Conference on Information and Knowledge Management.* ACM, New York, 621–630. DOI: 10.1145/2063576.2063669. 11

Salama, N., Aly, S.G., and Rafea, A. (2013). The use of social context to enhance mobile Web search experience. In *Proceedings of the 2013 International Conference on Social Computing.* IEEE, Piscataway, NJ, 92–3927. DOI: 10.1109/SocialCom.2013.143. 6

Salesforce. (2015). "Mobile Behavior Report." http://salesforce.com/marketingcloud (accessed February 8, 2017). 1

Sculley, D., Malkin, R.G., Basu, S., and Bayardo, R.J. (2009). Predicting bounce rates in sponsored search advertisements. In *Proceedings of the 15th ACM SIGKDD international conference on Knowledge Discovery and Data Mining,* ACM, New York, 1325–1334. DOI: 10.1145/1557019.1557161. 106, 113

Sellen, A.J., Murphy, R., and Shaw, K.L. (2002). How knowledge workers use the web. In *Proceedings of the SIGCHI Conference on Human Factors in Computing Systems (CHI'02).* ACM, Minneapolis, Minnesota, 227–234. DOI:10.1145/503376.503418. 15

Shen, D., Sun, J. T., Yang, Q., and Chen, Z. (2006). Building bridges for web query classification. In *Proceedings of the 29th Annual International ACM SIGIR Conference on Research and Development in Information Retrieval*. ACM. New York. 131-138. DOI: 10.1145/1148170.1148196. 4

Shin, C., Hong, J.H., and Dey, A.K. (2012). Understanding and prediction of mobile application usage for smart phones. In *Proceedings of the ACM Conference on Ubiquitous Computing*. ACM, New York, 173–182. DOI: 10.1145/2370216.2370243. 13

Sohn, T., Mori, K., and Setlur, V. (2010). Enabling cross-device interaction with web history. In *Proceedings of the International Conference on Human Factors in Computing Systems*, CHI, Extended Abstracts, ACM, New York, 3883–3888. DOI: 10.1145/1753846.1754073 1.2.1. 33

Song, H. (2015). Exploring the marketing value of mobile search: a case study on Dianping. Guangdong: Jinan University. 12

Spink, A., Park, M., Jansen, B.J., and Pedersen, J. (2006). Multitasking during web search sessions. *Information Processing & Management*, 42(1), 264-275. 4

Statista. (2017). Mobile share of organic search engine visits in the United States. https://www.statista.com/statistics/297137/mobile-share-of-us-organic-search-engine-visits/(accessed January 2, 2018). 1

Teevan, J., Adar, E., Jones, R., and Potts, M.A.S. (2007). Information re-retrieval: repeat queries in Yahoo's logs. In *Proceedings of the 30th Annual International ACM SIGIR Conference on Research and Development in Information Retrieval*. ACM, New York, 151–158. DOI: 10.1145/1277741.1277770. 15, 111, 112, 125

Teevan, J., Karlson, A., Amini, S., Brush, A.J.B., and Krumm, J. (2011). Understanding the importance of location, time, and people in mobile local search behavior. In *Proceedings of the International Conference on Human Computer Interaction with Mobile Devices and Services*, ACM, New York, 77–80. DOI:10.1145/2037373.2037386. 3, 6, 13

Tingting, J., Miao, W., and Huiqin, G. (2015). A search log analysis of OPAC users' searching behavior: a case study of Wuhan University Library. *Documentation, Information and Knowledge*, 167(5), 45–56. DOI: 10.13366/j.dik.2015.05.046. 6

Tsai, C.F., Lin, W.C., and Hung, C. (2010). Mobile web search by query specification: an example of Google mobile. In *Proceedings of the Computers and Industrial Engineering (CIE), 2010 40th International Conference on*. IEEE, Piscataway, NJ, 1–4. DOI: 10.1109/ICCIE.2010.5668288. 6

Tyler, S.K. and Teevan, J. (2010). Large scale query log analysis of re-finding. In *Proceedings of thee Third ACM International Conference on Web Search and Data Mining*, ACM, New York, 191–200. DOI: 10.1145/1718487.1718512 1.1. 15

Tyler, S.K., Wang, J., and Zhang, Y. (2010). Utilizing re-finding for personalized information retrieval. In *Proceedings of the 19th ACM International Conference on Information and Knowledge Management*, ACM, New York, 1469–1472. DOI: 10.1145/1871437.1871649. 105, 106, 113, 114

Tyler, S.K. and Zhang, Y. (2012). Multi-session re-search: in pursuit of repetition and diversification. In *Proceedings of the 21st ACM International Conference on Information and Knowledge Management*, ACM, New York, 2055–2059. DOI: 10.1145/2396761.2398571 1.2.3. 125

Verkasalo, H. (2009). Contextual patterns in mobile service usage. *Personal and Ubiquitous Computing*, 13(5):331–342. DOI: 10.1007/s00779-008-0197-0. 12

Vojnovic, M. (2008). On mobile user behaviour patterns. In *Proceedings of the Communications, 2008 IEEE International Zurich Seminar on.* IEEE, Piscataway, NJ, 26–29. DOI: 10.1109/IZS.2008.4497268. 6, 42, 43, 49Wang, H., Song, Y., Chang, M.W., et al. (2013). Learning to extract cross-session search tasks. In *Proceedings of the 22nd international conference on World Wide Web*, ACM, New York, 1353–1364. DOI: 10.1145/2488388.2488507 1.2.2 1.7. 14, 15

Wang, J., Li, L., Meng, F., and Zheng, Y. (2013). Empirical study of mobile searcher behavior based on Web log mining. *Library and Information Service*, 57(19), 102–106. DOI: 10.7536/j.issn.0252-3116.2013.19.016. 6, 38

Wang, Y., Huang, X., and White, R.W. (2013). Characterizing and supporting cross-device search tasks. In *Proceedings of the Sixth ACM International Conference on Web search and Data Mining*, ACM, New York, 707–716. DOI: 10.1145/2433396.2433484. 5, 14, 15, 16, 17, 23, 104, 116

Wu, D. and Liang, S. (2016). Research on the follow-up actions of college students' mobile search. In *Proceedings of the ACM/IEEE-CS Conference on Joint Conference on Digital Libraries.* ACM, New York, 59–62. DOI: 10.1145/2910896.2910921. 13

Wu, D. and Liang, S. (2015). A review of information search behavior under a multi-device environment. *Journal of Library Science in China*, 2015(6),109–127. DOI: 10.13530/j.cnki.jlis.156009. 79

Wu, D., Liang, S., and Ran, A. (2016a). Mobile search strategies of college students. *Journal of Library Science in China*, 42(3), 55–73. DOI: 10.13530/j.cnki.jlis.156009. 86

Wu, D., Yao, X., Dong, J., et al. (2016b). Designing mobile search tasks: a context-based approach. *Wuhan Daxue Xuebao (Xinxi Kexue Ban)/Geomatics and Information Science of Wuhan University*, 41, 34–39. 70

Wu, D., Zhu, M., and Ran, A.H. (2016c). How users search the mobile web: A model for understanding the impact of motivation and context on search behaviors. *Journal of Data and Information Science*, 1(1), 98–122. DOI: 10.20309/jdis.201608. 70

Wu, W.C., Kelly, D., and Avneesh, S. (2014). Using information scent and need for cognition to understand online search behavior. In *Proceedings of the 37th International ACM SIGIR Conference on Research and Development in Information Retrieval*. ACM, New York, 557–566. DOI: 10.1145/2600428.2609626. 128

Xu, Q., Erman, J., Gerber, A., Mao, Z., Pang, J., and Venkataraman, S. (2011). Identifying diverse usage behaviors of smartphone apps. In *Proceedings of the SIGCOMM Conference on Internet Measurement Conference*. ACM, New York, 329–344. DOI: 10.1145/2068816.2068847. 12, 13

Xu, X.Y. and Zhao, D.P. (2012). Research on the development of vertical search engines. *Advances in Future Computer and Control Systems*. Springer Berlin Heidelberg. 2012:579–584. 3

Yi, J., Maghoul, F., and Pedersen, J. (2008). Deciphering mobile search patterns: a study of Yahoo! mobile search queries. In *Proceedings of the International Conference on World Wide Web*. ACM, New York, 257–266. DOI: 10.1145/1367497.1367533. 4

Yu, F.X. (2011). Intelligent query formulation for mobile visual search. In *Proceedings of the 19th ACM International Conference on Multimedia*. ACM, New York, 861–862. DOI: 10.1145/2072298.2072494. 6

Yu, F.X., Ji, R., and Chang, S.F. (2011). Active query sensing for mobile location search. In *Proceedings of the 19th ACM International Conference on Multimedia*. ACM, New York, 3–12. DOI: 110.1145/2072298.2072301. 6

Zhan, K., Zukerman, I., Moshtaghi, M., and Rees, G. (2016). Eliciting users' attitudes toward smart devices. In *Proceedings of the 2016 Conference on User Modeling Adaptation and Personalization*, ACM, New York, 175–184. DOI: 10.1145/2930238.2930241. 133, 135

Zhang, Y., Liu, J., Qi, F., and Zhou, X. (2009). Mobile query expansion based on related word co-occurrence of abstract and log. *New Technology of Library and Information Service*, 184(10), 40–44. 6

Zhu, Y., Zhang, C., Xiaoming, Y.U., and Cheng, X. (2012). Query structure analysis based on PMI. *Journal of Information Processing*, 26(5), 33–39. DOI: 10.3969/j.issn.1003-0077.2012.05.006. 84

Zhu, X., Huang, J., Zhou, B., Li, A., and Jia, Y. (2017). Real-time personalized Twitter search based on semantic expansion and quality model. *Neurocomputing*, 254, 13–21. DOI: 10.1016/j. neucom.2016.10.082. 16

159

Author Biographies

Dan Wu (woodan@whu.edu.cn) is a full Professor of Library and Information Science at Wuhan University. She is the department chair of the Library Science Department, School of Information Management. Dan is the National Youth Top-notch Scholar of China, and the Luojia Distinguished Professor of Wuhan University. She graduated from Peking University with a Ph.D. in Information Science and was a visiting scholar at the University of Pittsburgh from 2006–2007. She is now a Fulbright Scholar at the University of North Carolina at Chapel Hill as well as the team leader of the Human-Computer Interaction Team of Wuhan University.

Dan's research interests span information retrieval, information behavior, human-computer interaction, and multilingual information processing. She has published 7 books and over 150 papers in important academic journals and conferences including *Information Processing and Management*, *Journal of Information Science*, *Aslib Journal of Information Management*, *SIGIR*, *CIKM*, *CSCW*, and *JCDL*, 21 of which are indexed by SSCI/SCI. She has been the Principal Investigator (PI) of over 20 projects, which are funded by such sources as the National Natural Science Foundation of China and the National Social Science Foundation of China. She serves on the editorial board for *The Electronic Library*, *Journal of Convergence Information Technology*, *Journal of Data and Information Science*, and *Data and Information Management*.

Shaobo Liang (shaobo_liang@outlook.com) is a Ph.D. candidate of Library and Information Science at Wuhan University. His research interests lie in understanding user information-seeking behavior, mobile search behavior, and cross-device search. He has published 13 papers in academic journals and conferences, 3 of which are indexed by SSCI. He has given presentations at several international conferences, such as JCDL and iConference. He is also a member of the Chinese American Librarians Association (CALA) and a member of the Association for Computing Machinery (ACM). He has received many honors including the Best Chinese Paper Nomination Award of iConference 2017 and the Chinese American Librarians Association (CALA) Scholarship for Excellent Student.